which?
essential guides

THE BRIGHT IDEA
HANDBOOK

MICHAEL GARDNER

Which? Books are commissioned and published by Which? Ltd,
2 Marylebone Road, London NW1 4DF
Email: books@which.co.uk

Distributed by Littlehampton Book Services Ltd, Faraday Close, Durrington, Worthing,
West Sussex BN13 3RB

British Library Cataloguing in Publication Data
A catalogue record for this book is available from the British Library

ISBN 978 1 84490 059 6

1 3 5 7 9 10 8 6 4 2

Although the author and publisher endeavour to make sure the information in this book
is accurate and up-to-date, it is only a general guide. Before taking action on financial or
legal matters you should consult a qualified professional adviser, who can consider your
individual circumstances. The author and publisher can not accordingly accept liability for
any loss or damage suffered as a consequence of relying on the information contained
in this guide.

Author's acknowledgments: The author would like to thank Alexandra Dixon for her
patience and support and to acknowledge the forbearance of his colleagues at Wedlake
Bell. Also, a big thank you to both Claudia Dyer of Which? and Emma Callery, my editor.

Project manager: Claudia Dyer
Edited by: Emma Callery
Designed by: Bob Vickers
Index by: Lynda Swindells
Printed and bound by: Stanley L Hunt (Printers) Ltd., Northamptonshire

Arctic Volume White is an elemental chlorine-free paper produced at Arctic Paper
Hafrestroms AB in Åsensbruk, Sweden, using timber from sustainably managed forests.
The mill is ISO14001 and EMAS certified, and has FSC certified Chain of Custody.

For a full list of Which? Books, please call 01903 828557, access our website at
www.which.co.uk, or write to Littlehampton Book Services.
For other enquiries call 0800 252 100.

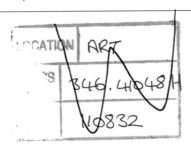

Contents

Introduction

Every year, many tens of thousands of people in the UK take the plunge and start their own businesses. Many of them dream of emulating the successful entrepreneurs, but it isn't enough just to have a bright idea. You need to know how to exploit it. This book aims to help you do that.

In 1903, a Yorkshireman called Percy Shaw left school at the age of 13 years. For the next 20 years he did a succession of odd jobs. He worked in blanket mills and offices, started and ceased an apprenticeship in the wire trade, tried boiler making and finally set up a business repairing roads. But in 1934 he came up with a brilliant invention that was to revolutionise road safety: the Catseye. Within a few years, his company Reflective Roadstuds Ltd was making and selling more than a million of them per year. Sir Percy, as he became known, would never have to work again.

Over 70 years later, a young computer programmer called William Gates created the code for a new computer operating system for the world's then largest computer maker, IBM. He sold his system to IBM for $50,000 but retained ownership of copyright in it for himself. The rest is history. Gates' company, Microsoft, still dominates the computer industry.

Both Shaw and Gates created brilliant products and had the business acumen to make them successful. But they may not have profited so greatly from their work, had they not taken effective steps to prevent others from copying and exploiting what they had created.

How did they do this? The answer is that they exploited the world of intellectual property, or IP for short.

THE WORLD OF IP

Most countries of the world recognise that creativity and inventiveness should be protected and rewarded so that such endeavours are encouraged. IP rights are legal rights that protect the results of such creativity and inventiveness. There are different types of IP rights: patents, trade marks, copyright, designs and confidential information.

Generally, it is the inventor or creator of the work in question that owns those rights and has the exclusive ability to exploit them. Hence Sir Percy was able to enjoy a monopoly for a period in being able to exploit his invention for Catseyes. He did this by successfully filing for a **patent** to protect his invention.

Bill Gates, meanwhile, retained ownership of title to the **copyright** in his computer operating system to prevent anyone else from copying it.

IP RIGHTS ARE IMPORTANT FOR EVERYONE

Gates and Shaw have become internationally renowned. Moreover, these days, we are used to reading about other famous entrepreneurs who have made it to the top through innovation, whether in relation to the provision of products or the delivery of services and the building of brands. Indeed, the growth and increasing importance of 'brands' has been another phenomenon of our age. Famous brands are always in the news.

But behind these high-profile examples, it is important to realise that IP rights are not just the province of well-known and successful businesses and their owners. IP rights can play an invaluable part in enhancing almost every type of business in one shape or another.

It is essential, therefore, that if you are thinking of starting a new business or have a new invention or business idea, you should be aware of what IP rights are, how they arise and what benefits they can bring. Equally, you need to be aware of the dangers of failing to protect IP rights – or failing to respect the IP rights of others.

Not everyone who invents something ends up as famous or successful as Sir Percy or Bill Gates. Nor, for that matter, will they necessarily become famous like the world's other great businessmen and women who have created successful brands and businesses from scratch. However, if you are seeking to develop a new product, process or service to put into business, you will find this book useful. In it you will find:

- An explanation of what the various types of IP rights are.
- How they can be relevant to your business and the exploitation of your ideas.
- How you go about protecting them.
- How you can enforce them.
- You will also find guidance to help you start the process of protecting them yourself.

If (as is advisable) you wish to instruct professional firms to help you with your IP protection, then Chapters 2 to 5 equip you with a basic grasp of how the law and processes work. They are written to help you in your dealings with the professionals. They will also help you to spot IP-related opportunities and threats to your business.

❝IP rights are not just the province of well-known entrepreneurs: they can be invaluable in every business. ❞

DEVELOPING YOUR IDEA

Having a bright idea and knowing how to protect any IP rights that arise is not enough. If you aspire to make a successful business out of your bright idea, you will need to finance your activities and bring that idea successfully to the market. For this, there are chapters aimed at helping you accomplish the following:

- Understand the various types of business structures (pages 110–13).
- Understand the various types of finance that are available (pages 114–22).
- Learn how to go about approaching investors or banks for finance (pages 123–4).
- Improve how you deal with pitching your ideas to others (pages 125–8).
- Obtain help in choosing a manufacturer or development partner (pages 133–4).
- Learn about pricing (pages 135–7).
- Learn about the importance of market research and how to conduct it (pages 146–54).
- Understand the principles of targeting your product or service (pages 155–62).

If doing everything yourself is too onerous, you may wish to look at other arrangements for implementing your invention or idea. You will find information about how the different business formats work including:

- Licensing agreements (pages 166–72).
- Distributorships (pages 173–5).
- Franchising (pages 176–7).
- Agents (pages 178–9).

FINDING OUT MORE

Inevitably, there is a fair amount of legal jargon to get to grips with. Wherever possible you will find that the emphasis in *The Bright Idea Handbook* is on explaining things in everyday language. To help you further, there is a glossary at the end of the book (see pages 203–9) together with a section of useful addresses for the bodies that can provide you with further information and guidance about many of the topics covered in the book (see pages 210–13).

There is so much that you can do yourself, and without spending a fortune. So if you have a bright idea, why not do something with it? It could be the best thing you have ever done.

Protecting your idea

If you create an innovative new product or come up
with an idea for a new service and want that venture
to be successful, in each case the product or idea
must be capable of being commercially exploited.
If it can be exploited, make sure that it is you – and
not someone else – who ends up reaping the benefits.
To ensure that happens, you need to be aware of the
different forms of legal protection – known as
intellectual property (IP) rights.

1

Understanding IP rights

When would-be entrepreneurs pitch for finance in the TV show *Dragons' Den*, they are often asked whether they have protection against their products or ideas being copied. Without such protection, there is often nothing to stop other companies with greater resources from stealing the new product or idea and producing and/or marketing it themselves.

If you are hoping to launch a new business, it is therefore vital to protect, if possible, your IP rights. The consequences of not doing so can be disastrous. For example, when James Dyson invented his now famous bagless vacuum cleaner and set out trying to sell the idea, he made sure that he protected his invention with a patent. Hoover was one of the companies that originally turned him down but later tried to copy his invention. Because he had taken the precaution of acquiring IP rights, Dyson was able to stop Hoover by successfully suing the company for infringing his patent (see the case study on page 25).

Acquiring IP rights can also be of great value to a business since they are assets that can be sold or licensed.

> **❝ Clashing – even innocently – with the IP rights of third parties can end up as expensive as failing to protect your own rights. ❞**

THE DIFFERENT TYPES OF IP RIGHTS

There are several different types of IP rights, some of which can overlap. For some types of businesses, many types of IP rights will be relevant. For others, only one or two of them will really be important.

Patents

A patent is a right that protects certain categories of new inventions that are capable of industrial application. For example, it could be a means of

 You do not only have to think about IP rights in terms of protecting what you have invented or created; the existing IP rights of others must also be taken into consideration. Clashing – even innocently – with the IP rights of third parties can be as expensive as failing to protect your own rights.

deactivating security codes on goods at a checkout, a method of manufacturing tyres more efficiently than before or a new type of drug designed to treat a particular illness.

Patents have nothing to do with copyright, designs or trade marks and exist separately from these other rights. For example, you cannot have a patent for a name or logo. Certain inventions are not covered either. For example, a method of playing a game cannot be protected by a patent.

To be protectable by a patent, an invention must be completely new. It is vital, therefore, that prior to filing for patent protection it the inventor ensures the invention is kept secret and is only disclosed under conditions of confidentiality (see pages 27–31).

Copyright

Copyright is a right that protects what are termed 'copyright works'. There are many different types of copyright work, ranging from literary works (like this book), films, artistic works, computer programs and databases to broadcasts and musical works.

Unlike some other forms of IP rights, in the UK at least, copyright protection does not require any registration or other formalities. It comes into existence automatically when a 'work' is created

> ### Database right
>
> **In the modern world, databases are extremely valuable business tools. Similar in some ways to copyright, database right protects the investment made in the creation of a database. It protects against the unauthorised use or extraction of data from a relevant database (see also page 62).**

that qualifies for copyright protection. This could be the text published on a company's website, a training video, photographs appearing in a brochure, the artwork on a piece of fabric or the recording of a speech.

The owner of copyright in a particular work has the right to stop anyone else from reproducing or dealing with the protected work without permission.

Trade marks

A trade mark is a sign (which could be in the form of a name, logo, slogan, sound, colour or shape), which serves to distinguish the goods or services of one business from those of another. For example, if you are in a shop looking to buy a television, the trade marks PANASONIC and SONY will distinguish televisions on sale made by these rival manufacturers. If you are listening to

For more information on patent protection, see pages 22–44. Copyright is looked at in more detail on pages 46-62.

11

advertisements on the radio, you may recognise the telephone dialling tune that accompanies adverts for DIRECT LINE insurance. When you are driving along looking for a filling station, you may see the green colour of the signage denoting a BP garage. When you order a bottle of Coke in a restaurant, the distinctive shape of the Coca Cola bottle will reassure you that you are ordering the real thing.

Trade marks can be protected by registration as a national, international or (in the EU) Community trade mark. The process involves filing an application with the relevant trade mark registry to cover the particular types of goods or services that the mark will be used for (see pages 80–6).

Designs

Designs are a form of IP right that protects the appearance of a product. Design protection can attach to an infinite variety of products, such as the shape of an air freshener spray, the design of an article of fashion clothing, the handle of an umbrella, the mesh of a fishing net. There really is no limit.

There are a number of different forms of design protection that are available in the UK, including unregistered designs (otherwise known as 'design right') and registered designs.

Registered designs give the design owner a monopoly over the design in question for a limited period of time (usually up to a maximum of 25 years). Unregistered designs have a shorter life span and protect only against copying.

Filing for design protection is relatively cheap and straightforward.

CHOOSING AN IP RIGHT

For a company manufacturing electrical equipment, like Dyson, all types of IP rights will be relevant. Its invention for making a vacuum cleaner work without a bag is protected by a patent. The registered trade mark DYSON protects the brand name. The appearance of the various types of Dyson cleaners may be protected by design rights and the brochures and information published by Dyson about itself and its products will be protected by copyright.

A company providing, say, counselling services will probably not have any invention qualifying for patent protection as such a company is unlikely to have any inventions capable of industrial application. But it would need to protect its brand with a registered trade mark.

Whatever your invention, think about what IP rights may be needed to protect your business, its products and brands. This should be done as early as possible before others try to muscle in.

The importance and benefits of trade mark protection are examined in more detail on pages 65–88. For more information about registering designs, see pages 90–108.

In Chapters 2 to 5 of this book you will find more detailed information about the different types of IP rights, how you obtain and protect those rights and whether or not they are relevant to what you are trying to do. Chapter 10 provides guidance on what to do if your IP rights are infringed by someone else and helps you to recognise where you need to take action.

WHY IP RIGHTS ARE SO IMPORTANT

If the invention or idea you have come up with is a bad one and has no commercial value, then obviously it doesn't matter whether or not you have protected your IP rights. Similarly, if you protect a great invention but you do not have the skills or ability to turn it into a viable business, then – again – you may be wasting time and money. But if you do have something good, then you will invariably be better off protecting your IP rights than if you do not. The following are the benefits of seeking proper protection for your IP rights.

Protection from unfair trading/copying

The recurring nightmare for any inventor or budding entrepreneur is that they think up something innovative and new and someone else ends up copying them and reaping all the benefits. IP rights can stop that happening. Indeed, they can sometimes be the only way of stopping that from happening.

If you do not ensure that you own and protect your IP rights, your invention, product or brand could be exploited by a third party without paying you anything. In other words, you could do all the hard work of creating an invention and developing it only for someone else to effectively steal all your hard work and creativity and make a fortune themselves.

Competitive advantage

Some IP rights have a limited term of protection. A patent is one such example, but for 20 years a patent can give you a monopoly on a product so that you have no competitors using the patented invention during that time. Once the 20-year patent period ends, with the right marketing and promotion – perhaps using other IP rights (such as trade marks) – you may have established such a strong brand identity for the product that even if others start selling their own products incorporating your invention, they will never be able to displace your brand's position in that market.

Adding value to your business

If you own IP rights to the exclusion of anyone else, you have a potentially valuable commodity that you can license others to use in return for royalty payments. It may be beyond your resources – and your business skills – to arrange for your product to be manufactured and distributed in the market. So instead of facing the expense associated with going it alone, you might have the option of entering into a licensing deal with a third party.

During field trials, the pharmaceutical company **Pfizer** discovered that the ingredient in one of its heart treatment drugs had an alternative use as a drug to treat erectile dysfunction in men. Pfizer filed a patent to protect its new invention and began marketing the drug under the trade mark VIAGRA. The drug was a huge success and VIAGRA swiftly became one of the best-known brands in the world.

Pfizer's patent deterred any rivals from marketing rival products using the same active ingredient. At the same time, the VIAGRA trade mark prevented anyone from naming any rival products using different ingredients with the same or a similar brand name.

But a few years later, Pfizer lost its patent protection for VIAGRA after a legal challenge by a rival drug company. The court ruled that Pfizer should not have been granted a patent for the drug. So the way became open for rivals to sell competing products using the same ingredients. The VIAGRA trade mark and brand name was unaffected.

By this time, however, VIAGRA had become such a well-known brand that it continued to dominate the market. Pfizer's product was obviously a hugely valuable one. But IP rights played a key role in Pfizer's commercial success. Patent protection had helped keep rivals at bay initially, allowing the VIAGRA brand to establish itself in the market.

This would enable you to contract out of all the risk and costs of taking the product to market. Instead, you would draw your income in the form of royalties from your licensee, which would obviously depend on the success of the licensed property.

Adding value to your business on sale

If you reach the stage where you wish to sell your business, a prospective buyer may be prepared to pay a higher price if you have protection for your brand or product names as registered trade marks than if you do not. If you have patent or design protection for your products, the competitive advantage this may give you will be another valuable selling point.

You may also need to think ahead of yourself. For example, if your business has the potential to expand into European markets beyond the UK, it might be a good investment to file for a Community trade mark (see pages 87–8). If you were later to sell your business and you had already secured the rights to the trade mark in the EU, that would be another feather in your cap.

For more information about entering into a licensed deal with a third party, see pages 166-72.

Protecting your IP rights

In an ideal world, you would always want to instruct a solicitor, patent or trade mark agent to advise you on the processes and procedures associated with protecting IP rights. However, in practice you simply may not have the funds to use professionals at every stage of the process or when you are first starting out.

By using professionals, you will have access to the know-how of those professionals working for you with the added bonus that if they mess things up, you will have someone to hold responsible and from whom to claim compensation. By contrast, if you do it yourself and make a mistake, there will be no one to turn to for compensation.

However, even if you intend to use the services of professionals, you will find it advantageous to equip yourself with an understanding of the basics. Copyright requires no applications or filings. The process of applying to register designs and trade marks can be fairly straightforward, patents much less so. If you know something about how the various IP rights work, you will be better placed to spot opportunities and threats yourself as your business progresses.

‹‹ An understanding of the basics will help you to spot new opportunities and threats. ››

USING PROFESSIONALS

There are a huge number of firms to choose from. How do you find the professional that is right for you?

Law firms

Commercial law firms usually offer a range of services encompassing such fields as IP, property, corporate, employment or private client services and litigation. A law firm will generally be your best port of call for drawing up commercial agreements for licences, distributorships, agency or franchise agreements. They are also likely to be the best for dealing with IP and commercial litigation.

If you are becoming involved in setting up a limited company (see pages 110–11) and have issues such as shareholder's agreements, again a law firm will be the appropriate place to go for relevant advice.

If you do not have the benefit of knowing any particular law firm or individual and you don't have any personal recommendation to go on, you will need to choose a lawyer from your own research (see pages 17–19).

Legal professional privilege

It is an important legal principle in the UK that people should be entitled to seek advice from legal professionals and to be candid with them without fear that these communications will be disclosed to any third party. Legal professional privilege is the term used to describe such communications. Where communications and documents are protected by such privilege they remain absolutely confidential between lawyer and client, save in very exceptional circumstances.

Patent or trade mark agents

Not all firms of solicitors have specialist teams who do IP work. Also, many firms that do have specialist IP departments may cover only 'soft' IP and so their practice excludes patents. If this is the case, there are two other types of professionals, besides solicitors, who specialise in patents and trade marks.

- **Patent agents** (also known as patent attorneys) are professionally qualified specialists in patent law and practice. They are experts at preparing patent specifications and making patent applications. A patent agent is able to talk to you about the process of applying for a patent and to give you an indication of the likely timescales and costs. An agent may also be able to help you refine the features of your invention that should go into a patent application (see pages 33–9).

- **Trade mark agents** (or trade mark attorneys), as their name suggests, are similar to patent agents except that they specialise in the law of registered trade marks.

❝ Don't be afraid to shop around. An expert trade mark agent may not be so good at dealing with a litigation problem. ❞

Firms of patent agents may sometimes include trade mark agents and vice versa, so if you choose a particular firm, you may be able to obtain advice on both types of IP.

 To read a fact sheet on using invention promotion companies, go to the Intellectual Property Office (IPO) website at www.ipo.gov.uk/p-advice-promoter.htm.

Choosing the right person for you

At the time of publication, it is intended that from 2010, new laws will allow firms of solicitors, patent and trade mark agents to combine in the same firm so there is the prospect of multi-disciplinary firms incorporating professionals from all these areas under one roof. But for the time being, you can choose to seek advice separately from any or all of these professionals, depending on your needs.

Depending on the law firm you are working with, it may be more cost effective to instruct trade mark agents to look after your filings of trade marks and to deal with oppositions to those marks, should they arise. Similarly, you may wish to instruct patent agents to advise on patent applications where a law firm does not have a strength in this area. As indicated above, it is quite possible, for example, that your chosen law firm may be strong in all types of IP work except patents.

With professional advisers it is often a case of 'horses for courses'. A good trade mark agent may be very good at filing trade mark applications and helping you with your filing strategy. But he or she may not be so good at handling litigation should it occur. So don't be afraid to shop around.

Jargon buster

Invention promoter An organisation that helps inventors to evaluate whether their inventions are likely to be commercially viable and, if so, to introduce them to businesses that might be interested in exploiting the invention

Besides lawyers and patent agents, for those who have invented things, there are 'invention promoters' who offer to provide assistance to would-be inventors to help evaluate and promote their inventions. Invention promoters tend not to be qualified lawyers or agents, rather they claim that as well as evaluating your invention, they have contacts with manufacturers and other established businesses who they can introduce you to. The Intellectual Property Office (IPO) advises would-be inventors to exercise caution in their dealings with invention promotion companies.

For more information about patent agents, a useful starting point is the Chartered Institute of Patent Attorneys (CIPA). Their website is at www.cipa.org.uk. See also the website for the Institute of Trade Mark Attorneys at www.itma.org.uk.

Tips for choosing and instructing a lawyer or agent

Follow this advice to make choosing and instructing a lawyer or agent as straightforward as possible.

1 Narrowing the shortlist

- Only consider approaching law firms that have specialist knowledge of advising on IP rights. There is no point in approaching your local high street firm if that firm specialises principally in wills, conveyancing or crime work.
- Look online. Most firms – particularly those who specialise in IP – have websites where you can find out what their capability is. There are niche firms, which are quite small, right up to the giant City firms. You can find lists of lawyers on various websites such as www.lawsociety.org.uk and www.lawyerlocator.co.uk. Likewise, the websites of the professional bodies for patent and trade mark agents can help you find suitable firms.
- Look at legal directories, such as Chambers or the Legal 500, which you can find at your local library.
- You are probably better off discarding the largest law firms. Go for smaller or medium sized firms instead. They will probably be less expensive and more likely to be appropriate for a new business.
- Draw up a shortlist of possible firms.

2 Making the initial approach

- With lawyers, telephone and ask to speak to someone in the IP department or to a named individual who specialises in IP. This will immediately give you a feel for what sort of a firm they are. If they are not responsive to your call, it may tell you that they aren't hungry for your business. The same would apply to a patent or trade mark agent.
- If you can speak to someone, sketch out who you are and why you need their services. Try to ask as many questions as possible and see how they respond. You need to feel comfortable that the professional knows what he or she is talking about and sounds interested in you as a client.

3 Meeting the lawyers

- Once you have done your research arrange a meeting with the professional of your choice to introduce yourself properly. Try to arrange the first meeting on a 'no charge' basis. This will enable you to size up the person and decide whether you would like working together.
- Law firms and other professionals have to comply with stringent anti-money laundering legislation so they will need to see proof of your identity to comply with these regulations and be able to register you as a client.
- Most lawyers and agents charge an hourly rate although for some work you may be able to obtain a fixed quote. You should be provided with details of their terms of business at the initial meeting. Good lawyers and agents will be happy to communicate with you about your costs as they go along.
- Make sure you keep tabs on the level of costs you have incurred or they could come as a nasty shock when you are billed.

4   Giving instructions

- Respond promptly and clearly, if you can, to your lawyer's or agent's requests for information. Try to avoid leaving long gaps between instructions or they may have to spend time reading back in to your file. This may cost you.
- Above all, do not withhold information from those you instruct. If you think information might be relevant, you ought to disclose it.
- Your dealings with your lawyer (and with your trade mark/patent agent) will generally be protected by legal professional privilege (see box, page 16). As such, the communications between you and your advisers are confidential.
- If you decide to instruct a lawyer or agent, you may be asked to provide money on account of costs up front. Depending on the amount (and your budget), you should, if possible, comply with this request as it gives you immediate credibility with your adviser and demonstrates that you are serious.

5   Building a relationship

- At the early stages of your business you will need all the help you can get and if you can establish a good working relationship with an adviser, you should receive valuable advice and counsel, without always paying for it.
- If you object to paying money on account, are difficult with your lawyer or agent or his or her staff, are reluctant to pay bills or complain about costs ceaselessly, it will do nothing for your chances of building the kind of relationship that can benefit you in the future.
- Think long term. If you can find the right lawyer, in particular, it will put you in good stead for the future. You should feel comfortable that he or she understands your needs and will take care of things for you.

6   If things don't work out

- If your chosen adviser misunderstands you or you don't feel comfortable relying on him or her, it may be time to look elsewhere.
- Despite what you might have heard, the market for legal services in the UK is fiercely competitive. As such, if you are a paying client, you do not have to tolerate second-rate service or excessive charges. If things do not work out with your lawyer or agent, there are plenty more out there who are ready, willing and able to take his or her place.
- If you decide to dispute the costs that your lawyer or agent has charged you, there are various options open to you. Ultimately, you could decide to take legal action but, wherever possible, try to use the firm's internal dispute resolution procedures. Be aware, too, that where your lawyer or agent has documents belonging to the case or matter, they may be able to exercise the right to hold onto those papers until after they have been paid all outstanding sums. You will find more information about what to do in the event of a problem on the websites for the various professional bodies referred to above.

KEEPING IN CONTROL OF YOUR IDEA

With certain types of IP rights (such as patents or designs it can be legally impossible to protect them if you haven't kept the details secret at the appropriate time. For other types of IP rights, such as copyright or trade marks, a failure to maintain such secrecy doesn't invalidate them. But you should still exercise care and discretion about publicising what you are doing – even to friends or colleagues. Whether you are planning to register a particular internet domain name or company name or to register a trade mark, you should make your application first before discussing it – just in case someone else beats you to it. Domain and company names (provided they do not infringe IP rights) are essentially registered on a 'first come, first served' basis.

Generally speaking, unless you need to tell someone about your proposed invention or business idea, then don't tell them! Get on and do what you need to do in order to put your idea into action and protect it first.

If you have to collaborate with other people, remember that they may acquire rights in what you are doing (see page 22). You also need to keep as much clarity as possible about who owns what.

 For more information about registering domain and company names, see pages 64-8 in Chapter 4, which is concerned with trade marks.

Patents

Most people have heard of the terms 'patent'
or 'patent pending', but there is a great deal of
misunderstanding about what patents are and what
they protect. If you have an invention and want to
exploit it, you will need to consider patent protection.
This chapter helps you understand what kinds of
inventions patents protect and how to go about the
business of obtaining one.

2

Obtaining patent protection

A patent is a particular type of IP right that protects inventions. A patent gives the inventor a 20-year monopoly on the protected invention. The state encourages new inventions and industrial progress in this way because ultimately this benefits the whole of society.

Part of the bargain between the inventor and the state is that in return for the 20-year monopoly, the inventor must make the invention public by filing details of the invention with the relevant government agency.

WHO CAN APPLY FOR A PATENT?

The person responsible for an invention is the inventor and that person is entitled to apply for the patent unless he or she has transferred the right to someone else. Where the invention is a joint invention and there is more than one inventor, those joint owners will be able to apply.

It is important to note that if an employee invents something in the ordinary course of his or her employment, then it is the employer who will probably have the rights to patent the invention. Under UK patent law, employees do, in some circumstances, have the right to be financially rewarded by their employer if the patent has outstanding commercial benefit.

So before considering filing a patent application, make sure that you really do have the rights to do this and that those rights do not belong to your employer. Otherwise, you might face legal action further down the line. You may even be sued by your own employer.

WHICH INVENTIONS CAN BE PATENTED?

The term 'patent' is often loosely referred to in the media. It is common to hear statements like 'they had a patent for the brand name Shell' or 'the design is protected by a patent'. In fact, patents have nothing to do with brand names or what things look like. Patents can only

 Give serious thought about the possible commercial benefits of your invention. There is no point in going to the expense of protecting an invention as a patent unless what you have come up with is something that can be commercially exploited. Just having a patent is no guarantee that it will be!

be granted for *inventions* that satisfy the following criteria:

- The invention must be 'new'.
- It must involve an 'inventive step'.
- It must be capable of industrial application.

What makes an invention 'new'?

You may think that your invention is new, but is it? The test for what is new is a tough one. Under patent law, an invention is only new if it does not form part of what is known as 'the state of the art' at the priority date of the patent.

❝ The test for what is new is a tough one. ❞

Jargon buster

Priority date This is generally the date on which the formal application for a patent is first filed with the relevant receiving office – it is the earliest date from which patent protection starts. The priority date is important because not only does it become the date from which patent protection starts, but it is also the date at which the validity of a patent is assessed. This is important if the patent is subsequently challenged

The state of the art In the case of an invention, this comprises all matter (whether a product, process, information about either, or anything else), which has, at any time before the priority date, been made available to the public (whether in the UK or elsewhere) by written or oral description, by use or in any other way. As 'the state of the art' covers the whole world, if something is already out there in, say, Chile, it can invalidate an application for a patent in the UK

Inventions that cannot be the subject of patents

Inventions consisting of any of the following cannot be patented:

- A discovery, scientific theory or mathematical method.
- A literary, dramatic, musical or artistic work or any other aesthetic creation.
- A scheme, rule or method for performing a mental act, such as devising a method for memorising lists of things using the creative and logical sides of the brain, playing a game or doing business, or a program for a computer.
- The presentation of information.

The above criteria, however, is subject to some limited exceptions. If you are unsure about whether your invention falls within those exceptions, you should seek professional advice.

Similarly, the following inventions cannot be patented:

- Those whose commercial exploitation would be contrary to public policy or morality.
- For a method of treatment of the human or animal body by surgery or therapy.
- For a method of diagnosis practised on the human or animal body.

Nigel comes up with a new invention for a novel type of bicycle lock, which he thinks could be a bestseller and is thinking of trying to patent it. He is on holiday in the US and befriends a group of locals. He chats away to one of them who is a keen cyclist, but who also turns out to be a journalist for the local paper. The journalist publishes a news story about Nigel and his ideas and mentions in the story the key inventive feature of the new lock and why it is so clever.

The result is that when Nigel comes to file his patent, it is no longer sufficiently novel – enough details of the invention had already been publicised in the US.

So if you invent something you think might be patentable, you must be very careful not to reveal it in public before the patent application is filed. If you should make the invention public before you are ready to apply for the patent, you will then have destroyed the novelty of the invention because your own disclosure can be used against you.

What constitutes 'an inventive step'?

As well as having to be new, in order to be patentable, the invention in question must also constitute 'an inventive step'. An invention cannot be said to involve an 'inventive step' if, having regard to what was known at the time, it would have been an obvious step to take for a person with skills in that particular area.

To decide whether or not something is inventive at the priority date and not 'obvious', you can apply an objective test using a 'notional person skilled in the art'. That notional person should have the following attributes:

- He has normal skill and is imbued with common general knowledge.
- He is assumed to have carefully read all the literature in the field, especially any relevant patents that have already been published.
- He is unimaginative.

Looking at the patent application through the eyes of that notional person – and avoiding the benefit of hindsight – you must try to assess whether or not your invention involves a genuinely inventive step that would not have been obvious to the notional person at the priority date.

It is important to note that just because an invention is relatively simple, it does not mean that it is likely to be held as not involving an 'inventive step'. The Catseyes road reflector invented by Percy Shaw in 1933 was a brilliant, but simple, idea that was protected by a patent.

❝ You must try to assess if your invention is genuinely inventive. ❞

Case Study | Dyson

James Dyson had patented an invention for a new bagless vacuum cleaner, which worked by exploiting 'cyclonic separation'. Cyclonic separation was not of itself a new technology, but the idea of applying it to a bagless vacuum cleaner was. Dyson tried unsuccessfully to interest cleaner manufacturers in his invention but he ended up creating his own company to develop and sell the vacuum cleaners.

Eventually, he had to sue a rival manufacturer for infringing his patent. They, in turn, challenged the validity of the patent and suggested, among other things, that it didn't involve an inventive step at all.

However, the evidence at trial showed that the prevailing mindset in the industry, at the time the patent had been filed, was against the idea of bagless vacuum cleaners. So, even though the concept of cyclonic separation was not in itself new, the industry mindset meant that the person skilled in the art would not have thought to apply it to making a bagless vacuum cleaner. Therefore, the attack on Dyson's invention as being obvious and not an inventive step, failed.

Nor will the patent fail merely because the basic underlying technology was already known about – provided the invention involves an application of that technology which is new and involves an inventive step.

Being 'capable of industrial application'

An invention is said to be 'capable of industrial application' if it can be made or used in any kind of industry, including agriculture.

❝ In the UK you cannot patent a method of doing business as such. ❞

Case Study | Neal

Neal attempted to patent a new automated method for acquiring the documents necessary to incorporate a company. It involved a user sitting at a computer and communicating with a remote server, answering a series of questions. The answers were processed by the computer and the relevant documents generated.

This was held by the English High Court to fall within the category of inventions that were excluded from patent protection (see the box on page 23). It amounted to a method of doing business and was a computer program, neither of which are patentable in the UK.

CHECK FOR A NEW INVENTION

Because a patent can be invalidated by the presence of relevant **prior art** anywhere in the world, there is always a good chance that someone, somewhere has got there first and what you think is a new invention has, in fact, already been invented. So how can you know? The answer is that you may never be able to tell 100 per cent. But you can help yourself by conducting some research beforehand.

- View relevant journals or books in libraries.
- Examine products that are already on the market.
- Use the internet as a research tool.

Of these, the most important and valuable resources are the internet services that enable you to search for existing patents and patent applications. The most useful one is Espacenet, which allows anyone (free of charge) to search worldwide for patents.

The Intellectual Property Office (IPO)

If you have the finance for it, another option is to instruct a patent agent to conduct a search for you (see page 36) or use the service offered by the IPO, who will carry out a detailed search. The IPO (formerly the UKIPO) is the government agency that administers

❝ There is always a good chance that someone, somewhere has got there first and your 'new' invention has already been thought of. ❞

To find out more about Espacenet, a database of patents worldwide, go to http://gb.espacenet.com. The website for IPO is www.ipo.gov.uk.

the UK's system of patents, registered trade marks and registered designs. It is the place where you file applications to register such rights and it holds a database of those rights that are registered. Most countries have their own equivalent to the IPO.

CONFIDENTIALITY

The essence of a patentable invention is that it is new and it also marks a departure from what has gone before. The novelty of a patent is not just assessed by reference to what has been invented in the UK or in Europe. The prior art extends to anything that has been publicised – anywhere in the world.

So to prevent the patent application falling at this basic hurdle, it is crucial to keep the details of an invention confidential until the application has been safely filed. Any revelation to a third party about the details of the invention before it is filed could potentially destroy its novelty – unless confidentiality is imposed. Only disclose details to the minimum number of people possible and only if it is necessary to do so.

Even after the application has been filed, keep details of the invention strictly confidential because it is not until the patent application is published that the public at large will know what the invention is. During the intervening period, you can take steps to find out if there is a market for the invention and whether it is worth incurring the costs of pursuing the patent application all the way. If word gets out about the details of the invention, it may damage those prospects.

Take care, too, with how you handle, transport or store details of your invention. If the details are on a computer, make sure you password-protect the relevant files and make password-protected back-up copies. Keep them in a safe place and make a minimum number of paper copies. If there is a prototype product, keep it covered up and secured.

❝ Even after the application has been filed, keep details of the invention confidential. If word gets out, prospects can be damaged. ❞

 Information about non-disclosure agreements together with a sample agreement is given overleaf.

Non-disclosure agreements (NDAs)

Both before and after filing the application, it is likely that you will need to disclose details of the invention to a third party, such as an investor or manufacturer, in which case you should use an NDA.

- Ensure that anyone who is told about the invention has signed an NDA (see the example, below).
- Do not disclose more than the minimum amount of information pertaining to the invention – even where an NDA has been signed.

When you come to visit a patent agent or legal adviser to discuss your invention, your disclosure to them will usually be assumed to be confidential. It would be a breach of their professional obligations to disclose details to anyone else. If you decide to see an invention promoter, make sure you have them sign the appropriate NDA first.

Sample non-disclosure agreement

CONFIDENTIALITY AGREEMENT

This Agreement is made on [ ]

BETWEEN:-

1. [insert name and address of party to whom you are disclosing information];

   and

2. [insert your name / your business's name and address].

(A) The parties are discussing certain matters relating to possible collaboration in developments arising from [insert your name]'s intellectual property (the 'Business Purpose'). These matters may require each party ('the Disclosing Party') to disclose certain information ('Confidential Information') to the other party ('the Receiving Party'). Examples of Confidential Information include all information whether commercial, financial, technical or otherwise, including without limitation all secret or confidential information of or relating to the Disclosing Party in whatever form supplied.

(B) In consideration of each of the parties disclosing to the other the Confidential Information each party has agreed to undertake to the other on the terms set out below.

IT IS AGREED as follows:

1. PROVISION OF INFORMATION

The parties hereto agree from time to time and in their absolute discretion, orally, in writing or in any other form, to provide Confidential Information to each other as is reasonably necessary for the Business Purpose, and subject always to the terms of this Agreement.

2. USE OF INFORMATION

2.1   The Receiving Party agrees to keep the Confidential Information of the Disclosing Party strictly confidential and save as expressly permitted under this Agreement not to disclose such Confidential Information to any other person, firm, corporation, association or any other entity for any reason or purpose whatsoever.

2.2   The Receiving Party agrees that it shall not copy (in whole or in part), utilise, modify, adapt, employ, exploit or in any other manner whatsoever use the Confidential Information other than as may be strictly necessary for the Business Purpose without the express written consent of the Disclosing Party.

3. TITLE

All Confidential Information of the Disclosing Party is acknowledged by the Receiving Party to be the property of the Disclosing Party and the Receiving Party acknowledges that all rights, including without limitation, intellectual property rights therein shall remain the property of the Disclosing Party and disclosure of the Confidential Information shall not be deemed to confer any rights to that Confidential Information on the Receiving Party.

4. RETURN OF CONFIDENTIAL INFORMATION

The Disclosing Party may require in writing at any time in its absolute discretion that:-

4.1   any Confidential Information and any copies thereof in whatever medium be returned to the Disclosing Party or destroyed (as the Disclosing Party shall direct) and may require a written statement to the effect that upon such return or destruction the Receiving Party has not knowingly retained in its possession or under its control, either directly or indirectly, any Confidential Information or copies thereof in whatever form and that all copies thereof in any electronic storage medium have been deleted, and the Receiving Party shall comply with any such request within seven (7) days of receipt of such request; and

4.2   any part of the Confidential Information which consists solely of analyses, compilations, studies or other documents prepared by or for the Receiving Party will be destroyed, and on request by the Disclosing Party such destruction will be confirmed by the Receiving Party in writing.

5.   EXCLUDED INFORMATION

5.1   The Receiving Party's obligations under this Agreement do not apply to, and the term 'Confidential Information' shall be deemed to exclude, any information which:

5.1.1   is in the possession of the Receiving Party prior to receipt from the Disclosing Party;

5.1.2   is or becomes publicly known, otherwise than as a consequence of a breach of this Agreement;

5.1.3   is developed independently by the Receiving Party; or

5.1.4   is received from a third party who is not subject to any confidentiality obligation.

5.2   The obligations of confidentiality set out in Clause 2 of this Agreement shall not apply to any Confidential Information which is disclosed by the Receiving Party to satisfy the legal demand of a competent court of law or government body, provided however that in these circumstances the Receiving Party shall advise the Disclosing Party prior to disclosure so that the Disclosing Party has an opportunity to defend, limit or protect against such production or disclosure, and provided further that the Receiving Party will disclose only that portion of the Confidential Information which is legally required to be disclosed and the Receiving Party will exercise its reasonable efforts to obtain a protective order or other reliable assurance that confidential treatment will be accorded to any Confidential Information required to be disclosed.

5.3 Except as provided above, the obligations of Clauses 2, 3 and 5 of this Agreement shall survive the completion of the Business Purpose or the termination for whatever reason of this Agreement and the Receiving Party acknowledges and confirms to the Disclosing Party that such provisions shall continue in effect notwithstanding any decision by the parties not to proceed with the proposed Business Purpose or any return or destruction of the Confidential Information.

Signed and agreed by the parties or their duly authorised representatives as of the date set out at the head of this Agreement:

Signed: _____

(Authorised Signatory)
For and on behalf of [ ]

Name: _____

Date: _____

Signed: _____

Name: _____

Date: _____

GET PROFESSIONAL HELP

Perhaps more than with any other IP right, it is very advisable to seek professional help and guidance through the patent application process. Patent law is a complicated field. The consequences of botching the application for a patent can be disastrous with regards to the inventor's hopes of profiting from that 20-year monopoly.

Unlike with applications to register trade marks and designs, patent applications involve much more detailed drafting work by the 'patentee' (the person applying for the patent). Although official fees payable for filing patents are relatively modest (see page 58), the greater complexity of patent applications means that professional fees payable to patent agents are likely to be significantly higher than those payable to advisers for filing trade marks or designs.

Also, along the way you are likely to have to look at earlier patents or applications and decide yourself or with advice, whether they affect your prospects of successfully obtaining a patent.

❝ For patenting your idea, it is very advisable to seek professional help through the application process. ❞

Patents summary: do you have something that is patentable?

In order to see whether you have invented something that might be patentable, you need to ask yourself the following questions:

1   As far as you know from your research, is your invention really new?
2   Does it involve an 'inventive step'?
3   Is the invention something that is capable of industrial application?
4   Have you kept your invention secret and disclosed it to others only under strict conditions of confidentiality?
5   Do you think that someone is likely to want to make commercial use of your invention?

If the answers to the above questions are 'yes', you may have something patentable and worth protecting.

You should therefore proceed to the next step of considering applying for a patent (see pages 33-9).

Applying for a patent

If you have answered yes to the five questions posed in the box opposite, you need to apply for your patent. This section explains the application process from start to finish.

FORM FILLING

The main things that you must be prepared for when applying for a patent are the number of forms to fill in and the length of time that the whole process takes. The UK's Intellectual Property Office (IPO) advises would-be applicants that a typical application for a UK patent takes three to four years to complete from initial filing to the grant of a patent. Once granted, the patent takes effect from the priority date so the period of 20 years will already have been reduced by the time taken to achieve the grant.

When you file a new patent application, you obtain a priority date for it, which protects you against any subsequent invention that may clash with your own. A delay in filing for protection can be costly, as the case study, right, shows.

Having protected your invention by filing it and obtaining a priority date, you are in a much better position to go out and explore commercial possibilities for the invention. You are also less vulnerable to losing your patent should details of your invention leak out. But bear in mind that at this stage you cannot actually enforce your patent against anyone else. You can only do that once it has actually been granted.

Case Study   Martin

Martin is a chemical engineer and discovers a new use for a chemical as an additive to petrol that improves fuel consumption performance by 5 per cent. No one but him knows about the invention. He secretly tests his new invention with an old car over three months to make sure it really works. Meanwhile, an engineer employed by BP makes the same discovery and his employer immediately files a patent application for the invention.

Two days later, Martin files an application for a patent. But he is too late. His invention is no longer 'new'. It has been anticipated by BP's earlier patent application. Since Martin had kept his own invention a secret, it could not be said to form part of the 'state of the art' at the date BP's invention was filed.

❝ The priority date is set when you file your application. ❞

33

Unfortunately, the grant of a patent does not mean that it will necessarily stand up if later challenged in court. When a patent holder sues or threatens to sue a third party for infringing his or her patent, the infringer will often make a counterclaim to try to disallow the patent. This will usually be on the grounds that it is not new or that it is not an inventive step. Attacks on a patent will often involve an intense scrutiny of its validity. Many such attacks are successful, as described, for example, in the case study below.

Both the IPO and the European Patent Office (EPO) websites provide samples of patent specifications for guidance. Another way to understand how a patent application should look is to examine some examples of patents online by using the Espacenet database.

❝ A counterclaim against a grant of patent often involves detailed scrutiny of its validity. ❞

Case Study | Sabaf

Sabaf was the owner of a patent for a burner for use with a gas cooker hob. The patented invention was for a particular type of burner, which drew its air from above the hob rather than below it. This meant that it was unnecessary for there to be fixings below the burner, as with traditional gas hobs, with the advantage that the hob could be much flatter on the work surface.

Sabaf sued an Italian company Meneghetti and MFI, the furniture company to whom the hobs had been supplied, for patent infringement. MFI settled with Sabaf, but Meneghetti counter-sued for Sabaf's patent to be declared invalid. Meneghetti argued that Sabaf's patent was not truly inventive in that Sabaf's invention would have been obvious to a person skilled in the field of hob design at the time when the patent had originally been applied for.

The case ultimately went to the House of Lords, which ruled in Meneghetti's favour and the patent was declared invalid. The court found that the invention consisted of using two separate, but existing, inventions side by side to achieve a technical result. Since those inventions were already known about, it was not an inventive step to put them to work side by side where they each operated independently to achieve a technical result. Although MFI were found to have imported the hobs incorporating the invention, even without the settlement they would have escaped liability for patent infringement because the patent itself was invalid and of no effect.

The IPO website is at www.ipo.gov.uk (search for 'Patents: application guide') and the EPO website is at www.epo.gov.uk (search for Annex III to the 'EPO's guide to patent applicants). The Espacenet website is http://gb.espacenet.com.

The UK patent application process

Typically, the patent application process takes three to four years from start to finish. The diagram below illustrates the process for making the application, which is also described overleaf.

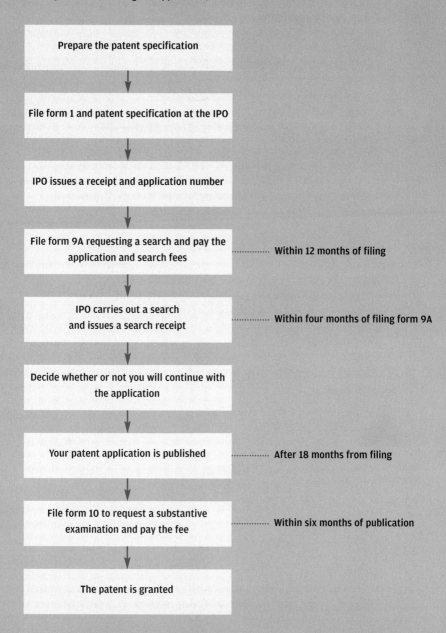

Prepare the patent specification

File form 1 and patent specification at the IPO

IPO issues a receipt and application number

File form 9A requesting a search and pay the application and search fees
············ Within 12 months of filing

IPO carries out a search and issues a search receipt
············ Within four months of filing form 9A

Decide whether or not you will continue with the application

Your patent application is published
············ After 18 months from filing

File form 10 to request a substantive examination and pay the fee
············ Within six months of publication

The patent is granted

The UK patent application process (continued)

1 Prepare the patent specification

- You need to prepare a document called a 'specification'. There is a sample on the IPO website, but the content depends on the actual patent application. It is in three parts:
  - **An 'abstract':** A short summary in no more than 150 words describing the salient points of the invention.
  - **A 'description':** This must be in sufficient detail so that it explains how the invention works and how it can be made.
  - **The 'claims':** Define the key features of the invention.

2 File form 1 and patent specification at the IPO

- Complete the application form 1, entitled 'Request for grant of a patent'. It is very straightforward and can be downloaded from the IPO website (www.ipo.gov.uk).
- If you are not the inventor, fill in an additional form (form 7) explaining why you and not the inventor has the right to a grant of a patent for the invention.
- Send the form (or forms) to the IPO, and by doing so you have officially 'filed' the application.

3 The IPO issues a receipt and application number

- On receipt of form 1 and the specification, the IPO issues a receipt. This has two important aspects:
  - It includes an application number for the patent application.
  - It confirms the date of filing of the application. This is important as it becomes the priority date for your patent application – unless you are relying on the priority date of an earlier patent application.

4 File form 9A requesting a search and pay the application and search fees

- The application fee is £30 and the search fee is £100. You have a limited time within which to file a search request in form 9A. This is up to 12 months from the filing date of your application or, if you are claiming priority from an earlier application, within two months of the filing date at the IPO.
- You must also pay the application and initial search fee at the same time.

5 IPO carries out a search and issues a search receipt

- The IPO examines the application to ensure that it meets certain formal requirements, notably that it is something that is capable of being patented. It also carries out a search. This involves the examiner looking for documents to see if your patent is affected by any prior patents worldwide.
- The IPO then sends you a 'search report' within about four months. It sets out references to any documents found by the search that could affect your patent's chances of being granted.

6 Decide whether or not you will continue with the application

- If, having looked at the documents cited, it turns out that your invention is not new or 'inventive', as you had thought, you might want to abandon the application before any additional expense is incurred.
- But if you do not think the documents cited really do affect your application or there aren't any other problems thrown up by the report, your application can proceed to the next step: publication.

7 Your patent application is published

- Provided no request to withdraw the application has been made, the IPO will publish the patent application after 18 months have elapsed since the application was filed. It is published in paper form by the IPO and is available from them or from the British Library. It is also published in the *Patents and Designs Journal*, which appears on the IPO website.
- This is the moment when the full details of the invention become public for the first time.

8 File form 10 to request a substantive examination and pay the fee

- Within six months of publication, you need to fill in form 10 to have your application substantively examined. This form, together with the appropriate fee of £70, is filed with the IPO. It is examined to ensure it meets all the requirements of the Patents Act 1977. If it does, you are notified that your patent will be granted (although this will not happen until at least three months after publication).
- If there are objections from the examiner, you will need to overcome them before the application can proceed (see page 38).

9 The patent is granted

- If there are no remaining objections to overcome and the examiner is satisfied that the application meets the requirements of the patents legislation, the patent will be granted.

❝ You will be sent a 'search report' within four months. If it turns out that your invention is not new, you could abandon the application. ❞

The fixed costs of filing for a patent application

Application fee	£30
Search fee	£100
Examination fee	£70
Renewal fees	£50–400 (increasing from the 5th year to the 20th year)

AMENDING YOUR PATENT APPLICATION

Once you have filed your patent application and you start approaching possible interested parties, you may find that you will develop or make changes to the invention or even improve upon the original. Or you may find that the results of the preliminary examination and search do not look very promising.

- **If you decide it is better to abandon the application,** you can always withdraw it. If you do this before the application is published, there is less chance of other people finding out about your invention and possibly appropriating your ideas for themselves.

- **If you do not want to abandon the application altogether,** you can file an

❝If you file an amended specification and there is no new information, it is backdated to your original filing.❞

Retaining your patent's power

Once your patent is granted, make sure that wherever possible, such as on the product itself or its packaging, in advertisements and marketing materials, you not only state that the product is patented but you also state the patent number too. This will improve your chances of recovering financial compensation against an infringer.

It will be very difficult for them to claim they were not aware that the product was protected.

If you are selling products in the period before the patent application is granted, you should use the phrase 'patent pending' to make clear that the patent has been applied for but not yet granted.

amended specification with the IPO. Provided that the amended specification does not contain any information that was not in the earlier specification, you can still claim priority from the existing priority date of the application. In other words, the date on which your amendment is filed is backdated to the date of your original filing.

- **You might want to file an amended specification** if you conclude that your earlier description is not good enough or if you involve a patent agent further down the line and he or she advises you to amend it.

ONCE A PATENT IS GRANTED

You may think that everything is sorted out once your patent has been granted, but there are still a few things that you should remember.

- **You need to pay renewal fees** for each year of the remaining period of the patent. If you fail to pay the fees, the patent will lapse (see the costs box opposite, top).
- **You also need to be vigilant to protect your patent** against abuse and infringement (see box, opposite, bottom). If you believe that someone has infringed the patent, you may need to warn them that they face infringement proceedings. If they do not stop what they are doing, you may need to take action against them (see Chapter 10).

❝ To protect your patent, you still need to pay renewal fees each year. ❞

Security

If, as a patent (or trade mark or design) owner, you need to raise finance and have to grant security to the lender for that finance (like a mortgage over a house), it is possible to grant security over the patent. This means that the lender would be able to take over ownership of the patent if you failed to meet the terms of its loan agreement.

Patents, trade marks and designs can also be bought and sold or transferred and licensed to others. It is important to ensure that any such transaction is registered at the appropriate office (the IPO in the case of a UK patent, trade mark or design), otherwise the transaction may not be enforceable against a third party. Also, until the IPO or other appropriate office is informed of a change of ownership, the former owner will remain the registered owner. The IPO website has details of what you have to do in order to register such transactions. The process is straightforward.

Filing for protection overseas

If you obtain a UK patent, you will have a monopoly on the use of the invention in the UK, including preventing anyone who has made products incorporating the invention overseas from importing them into the UK. But you cannot stop anyone using the invention outside the UK.

Nor can you stop anyone importing your patented product into the UK if you yourself put it on the market in another European Economic Area (EEA) country (the EU plus Iceland, Norway and Leichenstein).

To protect your invention overseas, you will need to consider filing for protection in other countries. This will increase the costs of the process in terms of filing fees (see the costs box, opposite) and patent agents' fees), so it is especially important that before embarking upon this process you make every effort to establish whether your invention is sufficiently valuable from a commercial point of view to make it worth the investment.

FILING OUTSIDE THE UK

There are three possibilities for filing outside the UK. You can file:

- An application for a European patent (EP) under the **European Patent Convention (EPC)**.
- An international patent application under the **Patent Co-operation Treaty (PCT)**.
- A national application in whichever country (or countries) you want protection in.

European patents (EPs)

Under the EP system, you can still make your filing via the IPO or directly at the European Patent Office (EPO) – as long

Jargon buster

European Patent Convention (EPC) The EPC was created in 1973 (and revised in 2007). It established a system of European patents whereby through a single filing, applicants can apply for a European patent that has effect under the national laws of any European states stipulated in the application. As at January 2009 there are 35 countries covered by the EPC

Patent Co-operation Treaty (PCT) The PCT is an international patent treaty that facilitates the filing of patents by applicants in different countries, via a single application to an administrative body. The priority date of a patent filed under the PCT is recognised by countries who are PCT signatories and the filings proceed as national patents in the countries chosen by the applicant

as your invention does not have national security implications, such as an invention for military use.

The result of a successful application at the EPO would be a patent that has national patent protection in the states you have designated. For example, if you filed for protection in the UK, France, Germany, Holland and Sweden you would have protection in those countries according to their national patent laws. The application process for an EP is slightly different to that for a UK patent (see the box, overleaf).

Filing an EP in a number of countries significantly pushes up the costs of obtaining patent protection overseas. Not only are extra fees payable for each country designated, but it is necessary to pay for the specifications to be translated

 If you think your overseas patent rights have been infringed, you will need to seek advice from professionals who are based in the country concerned. See also Chapter 10.

❝A successful application at the EPO would be a protected patent in your designated states.❞

into the language of each territory where the patent is to be granted. These fees are in addition to the extra costs of professional advisers.

The fixed costs of filing for an EP

The official EPO filing fees are higher than those payable for a UK patent at the IPO. The designation fee applies for each country you want your patent to be protected in. The others are the main fees payable, irrespective of which country you are applying to.

Initial fee on application	€100 (if filed online; €180 if not filed online)
European search	€1,050
Designation fee	€85 (€595 covers all countries)
Examination fee	€1,405
Fee for grant	€790
Renewal fees	Start from €300 for the third year and rise steadily to €1,350 for the tenth and subsequent years

In addition, you will need to pay translation fees if you are filing in non-English speaking countries, but these are not fixed costs and will depend on obtaining individual quotes from translation companies.

The EP patent application process

The process of applying for a European Patent usually takes around three to five years to complete. The steps are described below.

1 File form 1001 at the EPO with your specification and fees

- With the form, send a description of the invention, one or more claims for the invention, any drawings referred to in the description or claims, and an abstract.

2 The EPO examine the application

- An initial search report plus an opinion on patentability is issued with a priority filing date.

3 The application for the EP is published by the EPO

- Publication normally takes place 18 months after the application has been filed.
- At this point, the files relating to the application become available to public inspection.
- Publication creates provisional protection for your patent since you may be able to claim reasonable compensation for infringements that take place between publication and the date it is finally granted.

4 You file a request for a substantive examination

- You must do this within six months of publication and pay the fees for a substantive examination.
- You must also pay a 'designation' fee plus an extension fee if you want the patent to be extended to cover certain additional European countries, which remain outside the EPC.

5 The patent is granted by the EPO and news of the grant published

- The patent now comes into full force and effect in the individual countries you have designated in your application.
- You can sue anyone who infringes the EP, for the full range of relief available, including an injunction.

6 Period within which an objection can be raised

- There is a nine-month period after publication of the patent, within which a party that objects to the patent can file opposition proceedings aimed at blocking the patent registration.
- This can cause problems in practice. For example, someone might file an opposition to your EP and yet, at the same time, you might need to take legal action for infringement. Worse, it is possible that the EPO might reach a different conclusion about the validity of a patent to that reached by an English court. There have been signs in recent decisions that the English courts are doing their best to address these issues.

International patent applications

Another option for extending patent protection to overseas is by using the Patent Co-Operation Treaty (PCT) route. This involves filing an international patent application. The application can be filed with the IPO, the EPO or with the World International Property Organisation (WIPO) in Switzerland, which administers, among other things, the international system for filing patents, trade marks and industrial designs.

The application results in a priority filing date being allocated and an international search report issued by the receiving office. This provides an opinion about the patentability of the proposed invention. By 18 months from the date of your filing the application, you will have to designate the other countries in which you want your patent application to proceed. You then have to file certain forms in order to have the patent registered in those countries. This is known as the 'national phase' of your application.

Filing an international application has some advantages:

- **You do not have to make multiple filings** in foreign countries in the initial stages, but can work with a single international application.

 If money is especially tight, you may be better off filing for protection in the UK alone to start with. You will then have time to assess whether there is likely to be a sufficient commercial interest in your invention to merit the further costs of filing for protection in Europe. Provided your application for an EP or PCT is filed within 12 months of the priority date of your UK patent application, you can use your UK date as the priority date for the EP or PCT too.

- **The international search report that is issued** can lessen your costs and expenses and the administrative effort of filing in separate places.
- **You do not have to commit to extending protection** in specified foreign countries until up to 31 months from when you originally filed the international application. This then gives you more time to establish the commercial viability of the patented invention.

 Further information about the EPO and the EP system can be found at www.epo.org. There are various guides, information sources and FAQs on the WIPO website at www.wipo.int.

National applications

There is nothing to prevent you from making direct filings in the national patent offices of the specific countries where you want patent protection. However, this is likely to be more complex and costly than using the EP or PCT route because, in each case, you would have to file your application separately with the national patent office in question and in accordance with that office's own rules and procedures – and in the appropriate language. Where you file a patent application in another country, you will also need to have suitable local advice on the applicable laws and procedures that apply in that country. If you are interested in making applications for patent protection in more than one country outside the EPC area, then it would make far more sense to use the PCT route referred to on page 43.

The fixed costs of filing for a national patent	
Application fee	£750
Search fee	£1,500
National phase	Depends on how many countries you are applying to and varies depending on which national patent authority administers the process
Renewal fees	Variable, depending on the particular countries in which you choose to progress your filing in the national phase

Copyright

Everyone reading this book is almost certainly a copyright owner in their own right, whether it be through writing letters or taking photographs. However, businesses need to understand how the law of copyright works, not just so they can protect and enforce their own rights, but also so they can avoid infringing other people's copyright.

What is copyright?

Copyright protection is associated with the media, publishing, film and music industries and is a form of IP right that protects the original expression of creativity in most forms. However, its importance is much wider than that. All countries in the world recognise the need to protect copyright and have their own laws for doing so.

In the UK, our copyright law is governed by the Copyright Designs & Patents Act 1988, which runs to over 300 sections and numerous schedules – the details are best left to lawyers. The purpose of this chapter, then, is to explain the basics of how the law of copyright works, so that you can recognise what is and isn't protected by copyright and how copyright can be infringed.

THE NATURE OF COPYRIGHT

Unlike with registered designs, patents and registered trade marks, there is no registration system in the UK for copyright. No formalities or applications are needed to create or protect a work of copyright. Protection is automatic once the work is created and recorded in some permanent form.

Copyright gives the copyright owner the exclusive right to do certain things with the copyright-protected material and to prohibit others from doing those things.

Ideas versus the expression of ideas

Since a copyright work does not come into existence until it is recorded in writing or otherwise, if you think up an excellent idea for the layout of your new website, or, using a synthesiser, you create a catchy tune that you hope to use in a radio commercial for your business, but in each case you keep those ideas only in your head, they aren't protected by copyright law. Only if you record those ideas by putting them into some kind of permanent form will copyright law protect them.

Similarly, if your idea is at too great a level of generalisation, writing it down won't enable you to stop others creating something based on that general idea. One case that perhaps illustrates the difficulties in this area is the recent court battle over the *Da Vinci Code* where an author claimed that the book infringed his copyright because it took elements of ideas and themes contained in an earlier work.

Infringing copyright

When you visit a cinema and the film is about to start, the audience will usually be presented with a notice on the screen warning against any attempts to copy the film and that to do so will be a criminal offence.

Copyright infringement can indeed be a criminal offence. There are many forms of such criminal infringement, ranging from distributing pirated copies to using devices designed to circumvent copyright protection measures, such as modifying your UK DVD player so it will play DVDs bought in North America.

However, aside from the activities of counterfeiters and 'copyright pirates', when businesses infringe copyright, they will more often run the risk of **civil infringement action**. It can be expensive and disruptive to be on the receiving end of such action and it is all too easy for businesses to infringe others' copyright.

THE DIFFERENT TYPES OF COPYRIGHT

The copyright legislation creates many different categories of copyright 'works', each with their own set of rules. The types of such works are as follows:

- Original literary works.
- Original artistic works.
- Original dramatic works.
- Original musical works.
- Films.
- Sound recordings.
- Broadcasts.
- Typographical arrangements of published editions.

All of these types of copyright works have various rules applying to them, including the length of time copyright protection lasts. It is worth explaining a little about each type of copyright.

Jargon buster

Civil infringement action Legal action for infringement of copyright can be brought by the copyright owner against the wrongdoer in the civil courts. The kinds of remedies available in such an action would be an injunction, damages or an account of profits, where the wrongdoer has to pay over the profits made from the infringements

Literary works

For many businesses, this is one of the most important types of copyright work in practice. Literary copyright applies to such works that can be written, spoken or sung and includes letters, reports, articles, the script for an advert, the lyrics for a song, the source code for a computer program or a database.

So if you produce a product and write an instruction manual explaining how to use it, that manual will be a work of literary copyright. If you write text for your website explaining what your business is about, the text is likely to be a work protected by literary copyright.

If a surveyor visits a house and prepares a survey report, that report will

❝ Copyright legislation defines each category of copyright, and some of them have their own set of rules. ❞

be a literary copyright work. The text of this book is protected by literary copyright.

Artistic works

These would include graphic works, photographs, sculptures, architectural works, models, paintings, diagrams, maps, works of artistic craftsmanship and company logos.

Taking the example of the instruction manual referred to on the previous page, if there were diagrams and photographs in the instruction manual, those would be artistic works.

Dramatic works

These could be a play, a performance of dance or mime or a film containing some kind of 'dramatic' subject matter. For instance, a TV commercial could qualify as a dramatic work.

Musical works

This covers a work consisting of music, but exclusive of any words or action intended to be sung, spoken or performed with the music, which would be deemed to be literary copyright.

Films

A film means 'a recording on any medium from which a moving image may, by any means, be produced'. Film copyright can only be infringed by copying the actual images of the film. But there can be more than one type of copyright involved; for example, a film can also be a dramatic work.

'Original' works

For literary, artistic, dramatic and musical works to enjoy copyright protection, they have to be 'original' in the copyright sense.

This does not mean they have to have some kind of creative or artistic merit. It simply means, for copyright law purposes, that they must be the product of a sufficient investment of at least some original skill and labour by the creator of the work.

Slavish copies of an earlier work, such as a photocopy of a newspaper article, will not qualify for protection as an original literary work. Similarly a single word, such as a brand name, would not be a copyright work. However, a collage of brand names set out on a piece of paper might have sufficient 'originality' for these purposes to qualify for copyright protection. If a company name is turned into a stylised logo, it may attract protection as an artistic copyright work.

Questions of 'originality' rarely prevent a work from qualifying for copyright protection because the merit of any copyright work is irrelevant and the amount of skill and labour taken to give rise to copyright protection is minimal. For example, a photograph may be taken with the press of a button without any effort being made to frame or light the subject or to set the aperture or shutter speed, yet the resulting photograph still qualifies for protection. However, originality is very important in the context of assessing whether or not copyright has been infringed.

Sound recordings

A sound recording is a recording of sounds from which the sounds may be reproduced or a recording of the whole or part of a literary, dramatic or musical work – regardless of the medium in which the recording was made.

Broadcasts

These cover television (including satellite television) broadcasts. Content made available via the internet is not covered by the definition of 'broadcasts', except where a transmission of a programme or live event over the internet is being made at the same time as the TV broadcast.

Typographical arrangements

This type of copyright protects the appearance of the printed pages of published editions. It is a totally separate

---

Moral rights and performer's rights

An author's 'moral rights' are a kind of IP right protection associated with copyright. Such moral rights include the right to be identified as the author or director (as the case may be) when the work is published commercially and the right to object to the derogatory treatment of certain types of work. Moral rights are personal to the creator of the copyright work in question and can be waived by agreement. They have to be asserted before they can be enforced and only those to whom they are asserted are bound by them. They are also subject to a number of exceptions. For example, where title to the copyright work is vested in the author's employer, they wouldn't apply. In practice, moral rights of authors tend not to be that important, particularly in the commercial world.

Other types of moral rights are not just confined to authors. These include the right to object to being falsely attributed as the author of a particular work and the right to keep the privacy of photographs that were commissioned for private use. Although moral rights are limited, they can, in some situations, be enforced.

Performer's rights are another type of right created under copyright law. They protect the rights of performers from unfair and unauthorised exploitation. Performer's rights exist independently of other forms of copyright. Thus, a recording of a stand-up comic's performance would have protection as a sound recording for copyright purposes and the actual performance of the comic might have performer's rights protection.

For example, suppose that an unknown comic was performing a show at a club and Sam, a member of the audience, uses a camcorder to record the whole performance, without the comedian's knowledge or consent. Five years later, after the comedian had become famous, Sam decides to cash in by selling recordings of the comedian's early performance. Sam would own copyright in the film and sound recording that he had made so the comedian would not be able to sue him for infringement of those rights, but his performer's rights would still enable him to take legal action to stop sales of those recordings.

form of copyright to literary copyright. It can only be infringed by the making of facsimile copies of the printed work.

For example, the content of this book is, as we have seen, a literary copyright work. However, the book itself has separate typographical arrangement copyright as a published edition.

ASSESSING ORIGINALITY

Literary, artistic, dramatic and musical works all require an element of 'originality' to qualify for copyright protection. No such requirement exists for films, sound recordings and broadcasts. However, it doesn't matter what the content of the film, sound recording or broadcast is, it will automatically be a copyright work provided that it isn't a copy of an existing work. So for example, if you filmed three takes of the same scene in a training video, each of the films could have their own film copyright – what is actually depicted in the films is irrelevant.

OVERLAP BETWEEN TYPES OF COPYRIGHT

In practice, works of copyright will often overlap or exist side by side in relation to the same product or service. A good example of this would be a typical film DVD that you can buy in the high street. This may have:

- **Artistic copyright** on the cover artwork in the form of a copy of the poster or images that were originally used to promote the film.
- **An information booklet inside**, which again may feature an artistic work.

- **A piece by a film critic** in the booklet praising the film or providing a critique, which will be a literary work.
- **Typographical copyright** for the appearance of the printed pages of the booklet.
- **Film copyright** for the images of the film recorded on the DVD and dramatic copyright for the content of the film.

Because of the presence of multiple types of copyright work in one item, it is possible to avoid infringing one type of copyright, but to fall foul of another.

> ❝Works of copyright will often overlap in the same product or service.❞

Case Study John

John's company makes sales training videos. Sam sets up the same business and looks at one of John's videos. She decides to copy the content of one of the modules he has produced, but she recreates the module and reshoots it using her own camera and actors.

John cannot sue her for infringing film copyright in her video because she hasn't made a copy of his actual film – she has made her own film. But he can sue for infringing his dramatic work and literary copyright, since the content of the film is also protected by copyright.

Duration of copyright

This table sets out how long copyright protection lasts for each type of copyright work. This varies according to the type of copyright work involved. However, at the time of writing, moves are currently afoot at EU level to grant an increased protection for certain works, such as sound recordings, by extending the protective period still further.

Type of copyright work	Term of copyright protection
Literary, artistic, dramatic and musical works	• Expires 70 years from the end of the calendar year of the author's death. • Joint authorship lasts for 70 years from the end of the calendar year of the last joint author to die.
Films	• 70 years from the end of the calendar year after the death of the last of the principal director, author of screenplay, author of dialogue or composer of soundtrack.
Broadcasts	• 50 years after the first transmission of the broadcast.
Sound recordings	• 50 years after making the sound recording or, if published during that period, 50 years after the date of publication (new legislation may extend the term to 95 years).
Typographical arrangements of published editions	• 25 years after first publication of the published edition.

For more information about organisations that enforce copyright, see the websites for the Federation Against Copyright Theft (FACT) at www.fact-uk.org, the Federation Against Software Theft (FAST) at www.fast.org.uk and the Newspaper Licensing Authority (NLA) at www.nla.co.uk.

OWNERSHIP OF COPYRIGHT

As with all types of IP rights, it is very important to ensure that the rights are actually owned by the correct person. Otherwise, you will have problems if you come to enforce your copyright or grant licences to others.

Employees

As with most types of IP rights, where a copyright work is created by an employee in the course of his or her employment, the first owner of title to that copyright (barring a contract to the contrary) will be the employer not the employee. However, apart from the employer/employee situation, the first owner of copyright is usually the author or creator of the copyright work.

Contracted out work

Businesses frequently contract out their creative work to agencies or other third parties, such as for the design of a logo or packaging, brochures or other marketing materials. Under copyright law, where that is done the party creating the copyright work remains the owner of that copyright – unless there is a contract that says to the contrary.

Joint ownership may apply where more than one person contributes to the creation of a copyright work. So if more than one person – who is not an employee of your business – is involved in the creation of the copyright work, you need to make sure that they agree to vest their rights in you or your business. Otherwise, they will be able to restrict

Wherever you ask a third party to create something for you that could attract copyright protection and you want to own that copyright, you must ensure that you have a contract with that person. The contract must vest title to copyright in you or your business or you will not have undisputed ownership of the copyright. This is not necessary for employees because title will pass automatically if they create a work in the course of their employment. But for self-employed consultants, freelancers and agencies, it is essential.

your ability to use or license the resulting copyright work.

A COPYRIGHT OWNER'S RIGHTS

The owner of the copyright in a particular work has the exclusive right to do certain things in relation to that work in the UK. These rights are as follows:

- To copy the work.
- To issue copies of the work to the public.
- To rent or lend the work to the public.
- To perform, show or play the work in public.

Proving copyright

Although copyright ownership happens automatically, a copyright work may not have to be enforced until many years after its creation. Many companies and organisations struggle to prove title to copyright when they need to. It is useful, therefore, to have a system for recording when an important copyright work is created. This could be as simple as attaching it to an email and sending it to another email address so there is a dated record created.

Think about the important copyright protected works your business has. Would you be able to prove who created them, when they were created and how it is your business that has title to them? If not, you will make life more difficult for yourself if you ever need to enforce or licence the copyright.

- To communicate the work to the public.
- To make an adaptation of the work or do any of the above in relation to an adaptation.

Because the copyright owner has those exclusive rights, he or she can grant licences to others to do those things. Licensing of IP rights is dealt with in more detail on pages 166–72, but by way of a brief illustration, the case study below illustrates how copyright licensing may work.

❝ Many companies and organisations struggle to prove title to copyright when they need to. A dated record will help. ❞

Case Study George

George sets up a company that advises on health and safety matters. His business's operations include a subscription-based service whereby customers can pay to access health and safety instruction videos over the internet. His company also produces DVDs for sale and rent.

George decides to license the online rights to a separate online training company who are allowed to communicate them to subscribers via the internet. He also enters into a licence with a different company, giving them the rights to hire out his videos. Finally, George makes another separate agreement with a business books retailer licensing them to sell the DVDs. Thus, he has carved out his copyright to three different licensees.

53

Infringing copyright

The practical issues arising where IP rights such as copyright are infringed are covered in Chapter 10. However, businesses can only assess whether someone is infringing their rights, or avoid infringing other people's copyright, by understanding more about the law of copyright infringement.

CONFUSION ABOUNDS!

Just as everyone who reads this book is likely to be a copyright owner, so it is equally likely that everyone reading this book will have infringed someone else's copyright at some point in their lives.

For example, if you own an iPod or MP3 player and have copied tracks from a CD that you own onto your PC or laptop and onto your iPod, you will have infringed the sound recording copyright in the CD. If you have downloaded music from CDs you own onto your computer and then burned a compilation of tracks from those CDs onto a CD for listening to in the car, you will again have committed copyright infringement. Such 'format shifting' is currently illegal.

By contrast, if you have gone out to work and set your DVD recorder to record a television programme to watch when you get in, you will not have infringed copyright. The making of such 'time shifting' copies is perfectly legal.

In design circles, it is often said that if you create five differences between the original design for something and a copy of that design you make, then you won't be infringing it. Journalists sometimes believe that provided they copy less than 30 per cent of another article they won't infringe copyright. In fact, none of these so-called rules have any basis in law and should be ignored.

It is perhaps not surprising that there is considerable confusion about what people can or cannot do with copyrighted material. As a result, it is all too easy for businesses to infringe copyright and pay the consequences.

WHAT ACTS INFRINGE COPYRIGHT?

Since copyright owners have the exclusive right to do various things, copyright is therefore infringed when someone else, other than the copyright owner, tries to exercise those rights without the owner's permission.

 You don't have to copy or deal with the whole of the protected work in order to infringe it. It is enough that you have copied or dealt with a 'substantial' part of it. What is meant by 'substantial part' is examined in more detail on pages 58-61.

There are, broadly speaking, two categories of copyright infringement:

- **Primary infringement,** which is essentially a 'strict liability' category of infringement as it occurs irrespective of whether or not the infringer knew or suspected that he or she was committing an infringing act.
- **Secondary infringement,** which only applies where the infringing party knew or had reason to know that what he or she was doing involved dealings with infringing materials.

PRIMARY INFRINGEMENT

This can be committed by doing the following acts without the copyright owner's permission (remembering that in each case the act has to involve the whole or a 'substantial part' of the copyright work – see pages 58–61).

Copying the work

With literary, artistic or dramatic works, the copying can be in any material form. It does not matter how the copy is made. It could be by downloading it onto a computer, attaching it to an email, writing out a copy in manuscript, scanning into electronic format, photographing, photocopying or reading a literary work into a recorder.

Copying in relation to a film, photograph or broadcast, requires a copy of the whole or any part of any actual image of the work and includes taking a photograph of the whole or a substantial part of any image forming part of the film or broadcast.

So it cannot be an infringement of film copyright to shoot a new film incorporating identical subject matter to the original. This is because none of the images of the original film would have been copied.

Infringement of typographical arrangement copyright in a published edition can only happen by copying if there is a direct facsimile copy of the whole work or a substantial part of it.

Issuing copies to the public

Sometimes called 'the distribution right', this prevents anyone but the copyright owner from putting the original of the copyright work or any copies (or substantial parts of them) into circulation for the first time within the European Economic Area (EEA).

Case Study Andy

Andy runs a shop selling books, CDs, DVDs and games. He is visited by a sales rep from a distributor who offers him a batch of a best-selling book by an Italian author at a 30 per cent discount off the UK market price. The books are coming from a store in the US. Andy buys the books. He pays a deposit and once the books are delivered from the US he pays the balance and puts them on sale.

A week later he receives a letter from a law firm. The books he bought were put on the market in the US by the author's publisher there. Neither he nor they have given consent for the books to be sold in the EEA. Andy is therefore infringing the distribution right. He has to deliver all of the books to the publisher's lawyers and pay a hefty legal bill.

With so many goods available on the internet, you must (as a business) be careful about ordering goods from outside the EEA, which you intend to sell in the UK – unless you have permission from the rights holder to do so.

Renting or lending for commercial advantage

As this suggests, you are not allowed to rent or lend a copyright work (or a substantial part of one) for commercial gain without the rights holder's permission.

Performing, showing or playing the work in public

If you play a sound recording in public without permission you may infringe copyright in that recording. Similarly, other kinds of visual or acoustic presentation of something in public, such as playing a film, could infringe on the owner's copyright. There are, however, exceptions made in the case of broadcasts (see defences to infringement, bullet one on page 60).

Communicating the work to the public

This type of infringement was introduced to take account of the digital age and is illustrated by the case study, above.

Making an adaptation of the work

An adaptation could be any number of things. A translation of a work or a substantial part of it could be an infringing adaptation for these purposes.

Case Study Z Ltd

Z Ltd sells holiday insurance. Its marketing manager gathers together all the favourable press coverage it has had and (without seeking permission) scans the articles onto its website. Thereafter, visitors to the website can click on the 'Press' link and are presented with copies of all the articles. In this case, Z Ltd has infringed copyright by copying the articles onto its website. It has then committed repeated infringements by communicating the copies to the public and authorising members of the public to make further infringing copies of the articles on their own computers.

Turning a book into a play would be an adaptation. So adapting a work or doing any of the above things, such as copying, renting or distributing, in relation to that adaptation can infringe.

Taking the case study above as an example, if Z Ltd had put translations of the articles on its website and communicated them to the public, it would have been committing yet another form of infringement by communicating adaptations to the public.

❝A business must be careful about ordering goods from outside the EEA for sale in the UK. ❞

Authorising someone else to infringe copyright

It is not possible to get around the infringement provisions by having someone else do the infringing act for you. If you authorise another person to do it, you are equally liable. So asking your neighbouring business to photocopy copyrighted documents for you will not enable you to avoid being in the firing line.

SECONDARY INFRINGEMENT

This occurs only in cases where the infringer either knows or has reason to believe he or she is dealing with materials that infringe copyright. Such infringing acts include doing the following with infringing copies of the work:

- **Importing them** other than for private and domestic use.
- **Selling, letting for hire** or offering them for sale.
- **Exhibiting, distributing or possessing** them in the course of business.
- **Distributing them** otherwise than in the course of a business so as to prejudice the copyright owner.

Even being in possession of an infringing copy – provided it is in the course of a business and you have the requisite knowledge about its status – is an infringing act. It is very important as a business that you recognise the situations in which you might, unwittingly, be dragged into infringing copyright. Merely having some infringing copies of a work in a desk at work or on people's

computers could, if you knew about the material, make your business liable.

Further acts of secondary infringement are by giving permission for premises or apparatus to be used for the purposes of showing, playing or performing the work. For this type of infringement, it doesn't have to be an infringing copy of the work that is showed or played in public. For example, it could be a legitimate DVD of *Casino Royale*. It is the act of playing that DVD to an audience who have paid for admission to see it that is the infringing act – assuming the correct state of knowledge. Again, it is the person giving the permission to use the premises or who supplied the apparatus who is committing the infringing act if he or she knew, or had reason to believe, that there was going to be infringement.

Secondary infringement requires the infringer to 'know or have reason to believe' they are dealing with infringing copies. So, wherever possible, try to put people on notice by marking copyrighted material as being protected by copyright. This is usually done by using the copyright symbol - © - followed by the name of the owner/ author and the year of creation; for example, © Which? Ltd 2009.

'THE WHOLE' OF A WORK VERSUS 'SUBSTANTIAL PART'

Copyright in a work can be infringed where the infringing act is done in relation to the whole of the protected work or a 'substantial part' of it.

There is no difficulty in understanding what is meant by the whole of a copyright work. It means just that – the whole thing. Therefore, the copyright in a photograph would be infringed by the unauthorised reproduction of the whole photograph. If there was a magazine article protected by copyright, then copying the whole of the article would infringe. Recording a music track from an illegal downloading site would infringe.

Defining a 'substantial part'

In many situations, however, only part of a copyright work will be copied. Moreover, with the copying of literary works, there will often be an attempt to disguise the part copied by putting passages into the infringer's own words – so-called 'altered copying'. But however the copying is done, where the part taken from the original is a 'substantial part' of the protected work, infringement can still occur.

Unfortunately, there is no single test for whether or not something is a copy of the 'substantial part' of a copyright work and so infringes it. Instead, 'substantiality' is for the court to form a view on, based on the available evidence.

If you notice that a rival business has copied some of your copyright materials or if you are considering incorporating something from another party's material, you need to be able to form some kind of view for yourself. While this book cannot give you a definitive answer to what a 'substantial part' is, it is possible to equip you with an understanding of the important principles to help guide you.

- **'Substantiality' is primarily a qualitative test** and not a quantitative test. The key factor is not the quantity of the amount copied, but the nature of what has been copied.
- **You need to examine the source material** and identify to what extent it represents the original skill and labour of the copyright owner.
- **If a substantial part of that original skill and labour** has been copied, this is likely to be a 'substantial part' for infringement purposes.

In the real world, most situations where copyright is infringed won't be as straightforward or as artificial as the case study, opposite. But the same principle

Remember that just because you copy something in a different form from the original, this will not automatically avoid infringement. Copying, in any form, of a literary, artistic, dramatic or musical work can infringe it.

applies. In each case it is a question of examining what has been taken from the original and determining whether it is a 'substantial part'.

A good illustration of the 'substantial part' rule in action where a company logo was concerned can be found in the High Court judgment in the case of Handi-Craft Company & Others v B Free World Ltd (2007) EWHC B10 (Pat). In this case, the defendant (B Free World Ltd) was held to have copied a substantial part of the claimant's logo even though the copy differed from the original in several key respects. The judgment is published on the internet and is available to anyone via the website at www.bailii.org, where you can see illustrations of the original logo that was copied in the case and the copy that was found to be an infringement of it.

Using other people's copyright works

There are a number of instances where copyright laws allow you to do what would otherwise be an unlawful infringing act. Going into detail about them would

Case Study John and Brian

John decides to publish a book about Milton's *Paradise Lost*, which is long out of copyright. The text of the poem itself makes up about 80 per cent of the content of John's book. The other 20 per cent of the content is John's own written commentary on *Paradise Lost*. He is the author of that commentary. The book is published. It is a literary copyright work.

Brian takes John's book and uses it to type the Milton poem onto his computer for his own book. He does not copy any of John's commentary so he has not infringed John's literary copyright in the book, even though he has copied about 80 per cent of the content of John's book.

Although in terms of quantity, Brian has copied a substantial part of John's book, the material he has copied is not the product of John's original skill and labour - it is the product of the skill

and labour of Milton and the poem is out of copyright. So in qualitative terms, it is not a 'substantial part' for copyright purposes.

Suppose, however, that the facts of this case study are the same but that this time Brian does not copy any of *Paradise Lost* itself, but instead plagiarises significant chunks of the commentary that was written by John.

In that case, although Brian would have taken less than 20 per cent of the total text in John's book, he will have committed copyright infringement. This is because in qualitative terms he will have taken a substantial part of the original skill and labour contributed to the book by John. This example illustrates how the amount of material copied does not always determine whether infringement has occurred.

be impractical for a book of this nature. Besides which, unfortunately, for most businesses, the various defences are not especially useful. Some examples are useful, however, to explain the principles that may be applied:

- **You are allowed to have a television on in your establishment** playing live broadcasts to members of the public – as long as you don't charge for the privilege. But that privilege does not extend to the use of sound recordings, except for certain not-for-profit establishments like clubs, societies or charitable organisations.
- **If you are involved in court proceedings,** you can make copies of things for the purposes of the proceedings without infringing.
- **You can use extracts from a copyright work** to report on current events or for the purposes of criticism or review. **Incidental inclusion** of copyright material may not infringe in some cases.

But unless you seek advice first, the safest course is to assume that you

cannot reproduce the whole or a substantial part of other people's copyrighted material and to work on that basis.

CONSEQUENCES OF COPYRIGHT INFRINGEMENT

If you infringe copyright, you could be taken to court and subjected to a variety of unpleasant remedies. These include standard measures for IP rights cases, such as injunctions and delivery up of infringing articles. The remedies available are covered in more detail in Chapter 10.

When it comes to financial compensation payable for copyright infringement, there is a potential sting in the tail. Under UK copyright law the court is allowed in some cases to award 'additional damages' against an infringer. These bump up the compensatory damages awarded to the rights holder in cases where the infringements are especially flagrant. For example, these might well be payable in piracy cases where there is deliberate commercial copying of copyright works for profit.

It is also important to bear in mind that copyright infringement can be a criminal offence punishable by severe penalties, including fines or imprisonment

Jargon buster

Incidental inclusion This is where a copyright work is incidentally included within something. For example, you take a photograph of your partner in the street and in the background there is a poster advertising a film

❝ If you know that what you are doing is infringing copyright and still do it, you are straying into dangerous territory. ❞

Common copyright scenarios affecting businesses

Some of the more frequent copyright problems that affect businesses are as follows:

- Using unauthorised additional copies of computer software programs, such as Word, Outlook, Excel and Norton anti-virus held on a business's computer system, in excess of the number of licences purchased from the software company.
- Having copies of documents or other copyrighted materials (whether in electronic form or otherwise) brought by new employees from their previous employers and used for the purposes of the business they have joined.
- Use without permission on a website of third parties' logos, photographs or articles.
- Circulation of press cuttings or articles within an organisation without permission or payment of royalties.

of up to ten years. Although these provisions are largely aimed at serious offenders, such as those responsible for organised piracy or deliberate sales of such goods, they largely mirror the way secondary infringement of copyright works. So if you know what you are doing is infringing and still do it, you are straying into dangerous territory.

PROTECTION OF COPYRIGHT OVERSEAS

Copyright law in the UK is derived largely from domestic legislation, rather than European legislation. There are no equivalent Community wide copyright laws or rights in the same way there are with trade marks, designs and patents. Also, unlike with those other types of rights, there aren't any systems or processes for registering copyright to gain protection overseas. Instead, in most of the world, copyright protection arises

automatically, just as it does in the UK and your work is likely to be protected due to the effect of certain international copyright treaties.

If you believe that your copyright is being infringed in another country, you will need to consult lawyers in that country as there will sometimes be differences between what is protected under other countries' laws, compared to what is protected in the UK.

This book is therefore confined purely to looking at copyright law as it applies in the UK.

In summary, there is not much you can actively do – or need do – to protect your copyright outside of the UK. If you need to, you can rely on the automatic copyright protection your works will enjoy in most overseas countries under their national laws. But you would have to take appropriate legal advice in the country concerned.

COPYRIGHT IN DATABASES AND DATABASE RIGHT

Databases can be very important assets and are in widespread use. For example, you no doubt have a list of contacts you have built up in your email address book. That is a database. If you run a company, you may have a marketing database of customers. When you phone directory enquiries, they are able to give you the number you want by referring to a database of contact details.

Databases are protected by copyright and by a separate IP right known as 'database right'. They may also contain material that can be protected under the **law of confidence**. Note the following key points about databases:

- Where a database is created, it is important to ensure clarity as to who owns the rights in that database. For example, if a company employs an agent to sell its goods and the agent builds up his own database of business contacts, there is a danger that rights in the database may belong to the agent, rather than the company engaging him or her. That could be a problem if the agent were to start working on behalf of a competitor.
- If you find yourself using or copying from a database, be careful. You may be risking infringing copyright or database right in that database.

 As a general rule, assume that it is likely to be unlawful to copy the information from someone else's database without their permission. It is also possible that you might also be at risk of committing a breach of confidence if you start using information derived from someone else's database, again without their permission.

Jargon buster

Law of confidence A law that protects information of a private or confidential nature. This is information that is not, or ought not to be, within the public domain. Such information could be anything from trade secrets, medical records, sensitive corporate information about merger plans to information about a person's private life. The courts protect commercially confidential or private information from being disclosed or misused

Trade marks and branding

A trade mark is a sign that serves to distinguish the goods and services of one trader from those of another. For example, a red can with Coca Cola written on it tells you that you are drinking coke, whereas a blue can with Pepsi written on it tells you the drink is made by its rival cola brand.

Trade marks

A trade mark can be in the form of a name, logo, slogan, sound, shape or colour and as well as distinguishing the products or services of one business from those of a different one, it can also distinguish the identity of the business itself.

Examples of trade marks include:

- **The front of this book** displays the word 'which' with a stylised question mark after it. That is the trade mark of Which?, the publisher of this book.
- **The author's law firm** is called Wedlake Bell. That name is a trade mark – it distinguishes the author's law firm from other law firms.
- **If you stop at a Shell garage** (as opposed to a BP or Esso garage) you can buy Shell's V-Power brand of petrol, V-Power being the trade mark for a particular Shell petrol product, namely its high-octane petrol.

THE POWER OF A TRADE MARK

All businesses must have a name and all businesses must trade in either goods or services of some kind. Over time, if a brand is built successfully, it can acquire a value in itself and become a saleable asset or generate a profitable income stream through licensing. So from a trade mark perspective, even before you launch your business you need to ask yourself the following questions: what is the business going to be called? What is/are the name(s) of the product(s) or service(s) that the business will be trading in?

It is not just at the start-up stage that you need to think about such matters. Where you have already started a business and have decided to change the business's name or are about to launch a new product or service, you will need to decide what to call the re-branded business or the new goods or services you will be supplying.

CHOOSING A NAME TO REGISTER AS A TRADE MARK

Many businesses start by adopting either the name of the proprietor as their trading name or else adopting a name that describes the type of business they do. For example, a financial recruitment company may call itself 'Finance Recruiters' or a landscape gardening company may call itself 'Landscape Gardeners'.

The problems with adopting these sorts of names for a business is that unless the proprietor's name is relatively unusual (such as Anya Hindmarch), it may not help the business stand out from the crowd, at least early on in the business's development. Also, generic or descriptive terms that denote too closely what the business does can be impossible to protect as trade marks (see the case study, right).

So wherever possible, it is better to devise a name or trade mark that has a degree of inherent distinctiveness. A fancy name is generally better than a generic term. For example, a cereal manufacturer cannot trade mark the term 'muesli' for a breakfast cereal because 'muesli' is a generic term that describes a type of cereal comprising certain ingredients. However, it can produce a type of muesli and call it by the trade mark 'ALPEN' to distinguish its own muesli from the competition.

Domain name

Another very important factor these days that must be considered when devising a name for a business, or the products or services that it provides, is the availability of that name as part of an internet web address (known as a 'domain name').

If the internet is going to be central to the business, then choosing a suitable internet domain name is critical (see page 66). There is no point in devising a clever business name and trade mark for an internet-led business only to find that someone else is already using or has registered the suitable domain names you would need.

For many businesses, if customers cannot readily find you on the internet these days, your business is bound to suffer. It therefore makes sense for your

Case Study Geoffrey

Geoffrey, a solicitor who specialises in employment law, set up a practice called 'Just Employment' to provide employment law services. He also registered a trade mark for the mark 'Just Employment'.

He soon became aware that another party had incorporated a company called Just Employment Ltd. He sued for trade mark infringement, but the defendant company not only resisted the claim but also sought a ruling that Geoffrey's trade mark was invalid because it was descriptive of the services provided by him. The court dismissed his claim and ruled that his trade mark 'Just Employment' was invalid because it was indeed too descriptive of the type of services that Geoffrey provided.

internet address to match or follow your trading name if at all possible.

Company name

If you will be trading via a corporate entity, such as a limited company, you will also ideally want your registered company name to match your chosen business name. This is not generally as essential as matching an internet domain name and, provided you comply with certain formalities, such as displaying the business address and company number on business stationery and websites, it is perfectly legal to use a trading name for a company that bears no resemblance to the company's name as registered at Companies House.

So, if you can't register the official company name you want, all is not lost. But be careful. The fact that someone

Acquiring a domain name

A domain name consists of two parts: the name itself (which can be almost any combination of words, figures or both) and an 'extension', such as .com or .net. For example, Which? has the domain name 'which.co.uk'. A domain name is used to create an internet address, otherwise known as a Universal Resource Locator (URL). So Which?'s web address is www.which.co.uk.

You can buy domain names directly over the internet from a registrar. Registrars are companies that are accredited by the official bodies that govern the internet, such as the Internet Corporation for Assigned Names and Numbers (ICANN), which is a private, non-profit-making body that co-ordinates the system of internet addresses. There are numerous registrars to choose from, so shop around. You can choose simply to buy the domain name and nothing more or you can pay for the registrar to host a website for you. Domain names are relatively inexpensive and can be bought from as little as £10. However, they can only be bought for a period of time and will expire if the registration is not renewed. So if you buy a name for, say, two years, you will lose it if you fail to renew before the two years is up.

Most registrars have websites that let you search for possible available domain names. Simply punch in suitable names until you find one that is free.

The number of possible domain names has expanded hugely in recent years and continues to do so. As well as .com, .org and .net domain names, each country has a country-specific domain extension. The UK has .uk, for example. France has .fr, and so on. But beyond that, numerous new extensions are now available, such as .eu, .biz, .mobi, .tv and .tel. For a UK-based business, the best ones to go for are .com or .co.uk, since these are still the best known domain name extensions.

Domain names are allocated on a 'first come, first served' basis. So if someone has already taken the name you want, then it is no longer available. But if you think someone has registered the name in violation of your rights, there are ways of challenging their registration and seeking to have the domain name transferred. This could be by using the appropriate dispute resolution procedure for domain names or by means of legal action for trade mark infringement or passing off (see pages 76–7), if that is merited.

 For more information about .uk domain names, visit the website of Nominet UK at www.nominet.org.uk or www.nic.uk. For more information about domain names generally and for a list of accredited registrars visit www.icann.org.

has already registered a company with the same name as yours may indicate that they have got there first – see Avoid potential clashes on page 68.

CHECKING OUT YOUR CHOSEN NAME

Adopting a name that cannot be protected as a trade mark or which isn't available as an internet address can be frustrating and ultimately expensive. Re-branding in order to overcome such problems later on can be equally problematic and expensive. So it is always worth carrying out research before deciding on a name for your business and/or its products.

Fortunately, these days, almost everyone has the tools for that research available at home and at work. The internet is a fantastic tool for conducting such searches. There are four very simple (and free) types of enquiries over the internet that you can make to see if the trade mark or marks you have thought up are likely to be viable.

Trade mark search

This is very easy for anyone to do via the website of the Intellectual Property Office (IPO). Simply input the name you have chosen into the appropriate search field and the IPO database will show you all applications and registrations under that name – or that are close to it.

From there, you can quickly ascertain whether there is any scope for you to use that trade mark in relation to the particular goods or services that you need it for in the UK.

Google search

Obviously, by inputting your trade mark options into Google or other search engine you can very quickly get a feel for whether other businesses are out there who are using that trade mark or something similar to it – whether in the UK or elsewhere. You can explore the links that such a search throws up and look at the websites in question.

WHOIS searches

In order to find out whether you can register an internet domain name incorporating your trade mark, you need to make WHOIS searches. WHOIS is the common term to describe a search against a domain name to find out who owns it and a WHOIS database containing details of who is registered as owning all domain names is publicly available. For example, if you visit the website of Nominet UK (which administers UK specific domain names – see the bottom box, opposite), there is a WHOIS box in which you can type the domain name you want to search against. A search against the domain name 'which.co.uk' would throw up a

For an explanation on how the law of registered trade marks work see pages 69-79. The IPO website trade mark database is at www.ipo.gov.uk/tm.htm and the Google website is www.google.com.

record showing that Which? Ltd owns that domain name together with the Which? address, the date it registered the domain and the date of expiry. Useful databases for these purposes are Nominet for '.co.uk' domain names and a provider like Network Solutions for '.coms' and other extensions (see below).

Companies House search

The registrar of companies keeps a database, which is available free of charge to the public. This enables you to search for limited companies by name.

Avoid potential clashes

These four types of internet searches should give you a realistic view of how viable your chosen name or trade mark is likely to be. However, they also serve another – equally valuable – purpose. They may show up potential clashes with other businesses. In addition, if you see that someone else is already using the same or a similar trade mark in relation to the same or similar goods or services that you plan to trade in, you know that you will run the risk of having legal action taken against you for infringement (see Chapter 10).

APPLYING TO REGISTER YOUR TRADE MARK

By carrying out these free internet searches, you should have an idea of what options remain open for you in terms of your trade mark.

The next question is whether you should apply to register that trade mark – a process that will involve some expense and, in all probability, the involvement of a professional trade mark agent.

It is at this point, however, that you really need to understand more about how registered trade marks work and what are the benefits of registration.

While you do not need to become an expert in trade mark law, once you have a working knowledge of the main principles you will certainly find the process easier to follow and be able to recognise infringements of your rights. The following section is not intended to be an exhaustive guide to the workings of trade mark law, but it aims to equip you with the basic knowledge you will need.

 Network Solutions is at www.networksolutions.com. The Companies House website is www.companieshouse.gov.uk. See also the website for VeriSign, the body that administers .com domain names, at www.verisign.com.

Registered trade mark law

Once you have chosen a trade mark, you need to protect it, which is where the law of registered trade marks comes in. There are considerable advantages to applying to register your trade mark, rather than leaving it unregistered.

A registered trade mark is simply a trade mark (in whatever form) that has been protected by being registered in accordance with the relevant trade mark law that applies in the territory of registration. For example, UK national trade marks are governed by the Trade Marks Act 1994 and are registered at the IPO.

Trade mark law in the UK is derived from European laws made in Brussels, which have been implemented in the UK and all European Union (EU) countries. An EU Directive was made in 1989, which required all EU Member States to implement similar domestic trade mark laws. A further EU Regulation was made in 1994, which came into immediate effect in all EU countries creating a new type of pan EU trade mark right called the Community trade mark.

Registered trade marks are registered in relation to the particular class or classes of goods or services that the trade mark owner thinks he or she will be using the mark for. So it is possible to have different companies registering identical or similar trade marks, but for completely different types of activity. For example, Lloyds the insurance market has its name registered as a trade mark for various insurance-related products and services, while Lloyds Pharmacy Ltd has the Lloyds name registered for products and services that relate to the pharmaceutical trade.

The classes of goods and services are based on internationally agreed categories. A list is set out on pages 70–3, which helps you see which classes would be relevant to your business.

Registration confers various benefits on the registered owner of the trade mark, which you do not get unless you register (see page 76).

CERTIFICATION AND COLLECTIVE TRADE MARKS

There are also two other types of registered trade marks known as 'certification' and 'collective' trade marks. These are used comparatively rarely in practice and tend to be relevant to organisations such as trade associations or bodies that supply testing or accreditation services. Special requirements have to be met in order to register trade marks of this type. Further information can be found on the IPO website (see page 212).

Registered trade marks

You need to refer to this list when considering the types of goods or services that you want your registered trade mark to protect. Remember that each additional class costs extra in terms of fees.

Class 1

Chemicals used in industry, science and photography, as well as in agriculture, horticulture and forestry; unprocessed artificial resins, unprocessed plastics; manures; fire extinguishing compositions; tempering and soldering preparations; chemical substances for preserving foodstuffs; tanning substances; adhesives used in industry.

Class 2

Paints, varnishes, lacquers; preservatives against rust and against deterioration of wood; colorants; raw natural resins; metals in foil and powder form for painters, decorators, printers and artists.

Class 3

Bleaching preparations and other substances for laundry use; cleaning, polishing, scouring and abrasive preparations; soaps; perfumery, essential oils, cosmetics, hair lotions; dentifrices.

Class 4

Industrial oils and greases; lubricants; dust absorbing, wetting and binding compositions; fuels (including motor spirit) and illuminants; candles and wicks for lighting.

Class 5

Pharmaceutical and veterinary preparations; sanitary preparations for medical purposes; plasters, materials for dressings; material for stopping teeth, dental wax; disinfectants; preparations for destroying vermin; fungicides, herbicides.

Class 6

Common metals and their alloys; metal building materials; transportable buildings of metal; non-electric cables and wires of common metal; ironmongery, small items of metal hardware; pipes and tubes of metal; safes; goods of common metal not included in other classes; ores.

Class 7

Machines and machine tools; motors and engines (except for land vehicles); machine coupling and transmission components (except for land vehicles); agricultural implements other than hand-operated; incubators for eggs.

Class 8

Hand tools and implements (hand-operated); cutlery; side arms; razors.

Class 9

Scientific, nautical, surveying, photographic, cinematographic, optical, weighing, measuring, signalling, checking (supervision), life-saving and teaching apparatus and instruments; apparatus and instruments for conducting, switching, transforming, accumulating, regulating or controlling electricity; apparatus for recording, transmission or reproduction of sound or images; magnetic data carriers, recording discs; automatic vending machines and mechanisms for coin-operated apparatus; cash registers, calculating machines, data processing equipment and computers; fire-extinguishing apparatus.

Class 10

Surgical, medical, dental and veterinary apparatus and instruments, artificial limbs, eyes and teeth; orthopedic articles; suture materials.

Class 11

Apparatus for lighting, heating, steam generating, cooking, refrigerating, drying, ventilating, water supply and sanitary purposes.

Class 12

Vehicles; apparatus for locomotion by land, air or water.

Class 13

Firearms; ammunition and projectiles; explosives; fireworks.

Class 14

Precious metals and their alloys and goods in precious metals or coated therewith, not included in other classes; jewellery, precious stones; chronometric instruments.

Class 15

Musical instruments.

Class 16

Paper, cardboard and goods made from these materials, not included in other classes; printed matter; bookbinding material; photographs; stationery; adhesives for stationery or household purposes; artists' materials; paint brushes; typewriters and office requisites (except furniture); instructional and teaching material (except apparatus); plastic materials for packaging (not included in other classes); printing blocks.

Class 17

Rubber, gutta-percha, gum, asbestos, mica and goods made from these materials and not included in other classes; plastics in extruded form for use in manufacture; packing, stopping and insulating materials; flexible pipes, not of metal.

Class 18

Leather and imitations of leather, and goods made of these materials and not included in other classes; animal skins, hides; trunks and travelling bags; umbrellas, parasols and walking sticks; whips, harness and saddlery.

Class 19

Building materials (non-metallic); non-metallic rigid pipes for building; asphalt, pitch and bitumen; non-metallic transportable buildings; monuments, not of metal.

Class 20

Furniture, mirrors, picture frames; goods (not included in other classes) of wood, cork, reed, cane, wicker, horn, bone, ivory, whalebone, shell, amber, mother-of-pearl, meerschaum and substitutes for all these materials, or of plastics.

❝ There are different classes of registered trade mark according to the types of goods or services that are to be protected. ❞

Class 21

Household or kitchen utensils and containers; combs and sponges; brushes (except paint brushes); brush-making materials; articles for cleaning purposes; steelwool; unworked or semi-worked glass (except glass used in building); glassware, porcelain and earthenware not included in other classes.

Class 22

Ropes, string, nets, tents, awnings, tarpaulins, sails, sacks and bags (not included in other classes); padding and stuffing materials (except of rubber or plastics); raw fibrous textile materials.

Class 23

Yarns and threads, for textile use.

Class 24

Textiles and textile goods, not included in other classes; bed and table covers.

Class 25

Clothing, footwear, headgear.

Class 26

Lace and embroidery, ribbons and braid; buttons, hooks and eyes, pins and needles; artificial flowers.

Class 27

Carpets, rugs, mats and matting, linoleum and other materials for covering existing floors; wall hangings (non-textile).

Class 28

Games and playthings; gymnastic and sporting articles not included in other classes; decorations for Christmas trees.

Class 29

Meat, fish, poultry and game; meat extracts; preserved, frozen, dried and cooked fruits and vegetables; jellies, jams, compotes; eggs, milk and milk products; edible oils and fats.

Class 30

Coffee, tea, cocoa, sugar, rice, tapioca, sago, artificial coffee; flour and preparations made from cereals, bread, pastry and confectionery, ices; honey, treacle; yeast, baking-powder; salt, mustard; vinegar, sauces (condiments); spices; ice.

Class 31

Agricultural, horticultural and forestry products and grains not included in other classes; live animals; fresh fruits and vegetables; seeds, natural plants and flowers; foodstuffs for animals, malt.

Class 32

Beers; mineral and aerated waters and other non-alcoholic drinks; fruit drinks and fruit juices; syrups and other preparations for making beverages.

Class 33

Alcoholic beverages (except beers).

Class 34

Tobacco; smokers' articles; matches.

Class 35

Advertising; business management; business administration; office functions.

Class 36

Insurance; financial affairs; monetary affairs; real estate affairs.

Class 37

Building construction; repair; installation services.

Class 38

Telecommunications.

Class 39

Transport; packaging and storage of goods; travel arrangement.

Class 40

Treatment of materials.

Class 41

Education; providing of training; entertainment; sporting and cultural activities.

Class 42

Scientific and technological services and research and design relating thereto; industrial analysis and research services; design and development of computer hardware and software.

Class 43

Services for providing food and drink; temporary accommodation.

Class 44

Medical services; veterinary services; hygienic and beauty care for human beings or animals; agriculture, horticulture and forestry services.

Class 45

Legal services; security services for the protection of property and individuals; personal and social services rendered by others to meet the needs of individuals.

❝ You will have to pay separate fees for each class in which you wish to obtain trade mark protection. ❞

 The steps that you need to take in order to register your trade mark are described on pages 80-6.

TRADE MARKS THAT CAN BE REGISTERED

To be capable of registration as a trade mark, a sign must meet the compulsory requirements of the trade marks legislation. If it does not do so, your application to register the mark will not even get off the ground. So it is worth being aware of these. Absolute requirements for registration are that the sign:

- **Must be capable of being represented graphically,** so words, logos, packaging, shapes, sounds (using notation) and colours (by reference to internationally recognised colour codes) are all registerable, whereas a smell, for example, is not.
- **Must be capable of distinguishing the goods** or services of one undertaking from those of another; for example, 'muesli' for breakfast cereals is a no-no; Alpen for breakfast cereals is fine.

Signs cannot be registered when they:

- Are devoid of distinctive character, such as aspirin.
- Consist of signs or indications that describe only the purpose, value or characteristics of the goods or services, such as the Mobile Phone Shop for a shop selling mobile phones.
- Consist of signs or indications that have become customary in the current language or in the established practices of the trade, such as decaf for decaffeinated coffee. (Note, however, that if the applicant can show that the sign has become distinctive through the use made of it, this can make the mark registerable after all.)

- **Consist exclusively of shapes** resulting from a) the nature of the goods themselves, or b) where the shape is necessary to achieve a technical result, or c) where the shape gives 'substantial value' to the goods. Perhaps the best example of recent times is the litigation in relation to (b) where the courts in the UK have held that the shape of the three-headed razor made by Philips cannot be a valid trade mark.
- **Are contrary to public policy** or accepted principles of morality or signs that are deceptive to the public. Examples of trade marks that might have fallen into this category but have been accepted for registration in the UK are FCUK and NO F IN JUSTICE.
- **Clash with 'specially protected emblems',** such as Royal arms, Olympic symbols and pictures of the Queen.

The law relating to shape marks is a rather complicated area of trade mark law that is beyond the scope of this book. If you have a shape that you want to register, get advice from a professional, such as a lawyer or trade mark agent.

There are also another set of important grounds (known as 'relative grounds') on which applications to register trade marks may fail. These include where the proposed mark clashes with a mark already registered (if it is too similar to it or takes unfair advantage of it), or where another party already has a right in the mark applied for, such as the right to sue for passing off. Objections based on such 'relative grounds' are often the basis for third parties to oppose the granting of trade mark applications where they fear the application may harm their own trade marks.

THE PROS AND CONS OF REGISTERING YOUR TRADE MARK

It is not compulsory to have a trade mark registered. But failing to register it deprives the trade mark owner of the benefits of registration.

Creating a monopoly

Registration of a trade mark creates a monopoly (potentially indefinite) in favour of the trade mark owner, for the use of the trade mark in relation to the goods or services specified in the registration. Like a patent or a design, a registered trade mark can be transferred or sold, licensed or used as security.

Acquisition of positive and negative rights

In addition, by registering your trade mark you get positive rights (the exclusive right to use, or license others to use, the mark) and negative rights (the right to

stop unauthorised use of the mark by third parties). For example, the brand owner Rolex has a registration for the trade mark ROLEX. As such, it has the exclusive right to use the mark ROLEX on watches imported, advertised for sale or sold in the UK. If any other trader attempts – without a licence – to use an identical sign on watches, they would be infringing the ROLEX trade mark, unless they were watches Rolex itself had previously put on the EEA market.

But that is not the full extent of the monopoly the trade mark has once your mark is registered. Even a sign that is not identical to the trade mark, but only similar to it, can potentially infringe the trade mark registration – provided that there is a likelihood of confusion between the offending sign and the trade mark; for example, a watch called a Rollex

Case Study **AN**

AN, a newspaper publisher, had registered trade marks for THE MAIL, THE DAILY MAIL and THE MAIL ON SUNDAY. EN, a rival publisher, proposed to introduce a newspaper called either *The London Evening Mail* or *The Evening Mail*. AN sued EN for trade mark infringement.

The Court held that there was similarity between AN's registered trade marks and the proposed names of EN's newspapers and there was a likelihood of confusion between them. The trade marks were therefore infringed.

Trade marks and branding

would almost certainly infringe the ROLEX mark.

Protection for well-known brands

Where a particular trade mark is famous or has acquired a 'reputation', the rights of the registered trade mark owner are even wider. Where the trade mark has a 'reputation', infringement can occur even if the offending trader's sign is being used in relation to completely different goods or services to those for which the trade mark owner has registered the mark.

> ❝ The right to sue for passing off is a remedy for protecting against damage to a business's goodwill. ❞

To succeed in showing infringement under this provision, the trade mark owner has to establish that the sign is being used 'without due cause' and that it takes unfair advantage of, or is detrimental to, the distinctive character or reputation of the registered trade mark (see page 184).

Passing off

If a trade mark is not registered, then if another trader causes damage to the trade mark owner by using the same or a similar trade mark, the injured party has to rely on a claim of 'passing off' to stop the offending activity.

The right to sue for passing off is a remedy for protecting against damage to a business's goodwill. It can be used as an additional claim where there is registered trade mark infringement. Or if there is no registered mark, suing

---

Case Study | **Elogicom Ltd**

Elogicom Ltd registered a number of internet domain names incorporating the name of the well-known supermarket retailer Tesco. These domain names were used by Elogicorm to drive internet traffic to Tesco's own websites, but via an internet affiliate marketing company – Tradedoubler – with whom Tesco had an arrangement. As a result, Tesco was obliged to pay commission to Elogicom via Tradedoubler.

Tesco objected to the use of the domain names incorporating its

registered trade marks for the mark TESCO. It claimed, among other things, that Elogicom was taking unfair advantage of the reputation of the Tesco trade marks by using them in domain names. It was, in effect, as if Elogicom was standing at the entrance of every Tesco store charging Tesco for each customer going through the door.

The court agreed that Elogicom had infringed Tesco's trade marks by taking unfair advantage of them.

for passing off will often be the only claim available.

An example of passing off is the sale by a retailer of counterfeit Nike T-shirts. Nike have a goodwill and reputation in the UK by reference to the 'Nike' name and 'swish' trade mark. If someone sells fake Nike T-shirts, they are falsely representing to others that their goods are from Nike when they aren't. This is passing off.

For a claim of passing off to succeed, the claimant must be able to show the following three things:

- That it has a sufficient goodwill and reputation in the UK by reference to the particular trade mark, such as its name or logo. This is something that can only be built up by trading in the UK.
- The claimant must show that another trader is using the same or a similar sign to the identifying trade mark so as to misrepresent to consumers or traders that it or its goods or services are supplied by the claimant or associated in trade with the claimant – when, in fact, that is not the case.
- The claimant must show that the misrepresentation is causing or will cause it damage. This last point will often follow on naturally from the second factor.

The right to sue for passing off is only available to traders who have managed to build up a sufficient goodwill and recognition in the UK by reference to their particular trade mark or identifying feature. So it is of no help to many new businesses in their early stages, which haven't traded long enough to create that goodwill. As a new business it is therefore always best to apply to register your trade mark as soon as possible so as to establish clearly the primacy of your rights to a particular trade mark.

Case Study Colin

Colin has an idea for an internet-based business providing a centralised booking system for taxis. He calls his business 'borataxis.com'. He buys the domain name borataxis.com and pays an internet consultant to design him a website. He prints stationary with his new company name on it and starts trading.

But three weeks later he notices that a rival, Bert, has just set up a similar website at www.borataxis.co.uk. Colin sues Bert for passing off, but because his name isn't registered and nor can he show that in the short time he has been trading he has built up sufficient goodwill and reputation by reference to the trading name borataxis.com, Colin cannot immediately stop Bert from using the trading name Borataxis. If he had filed an application to register the name Borataxis as a trade mark, he would have had priority rights over the name and could ultimately have been able to stop Bert from using the name too.

The pros and cons of trade mark registration

Pros

- You have the exclusive right to use the trade mark in relation to the goods or services for which it is registered. This right may potentially be renewable indefinitely.
- You have the rights to prevent others from registering or using trade marks that are confusingly similar to yours in relation to the same or similar goods or services.
- If your trade mark becomes sufficiently well known, you have even wider rights to block registrations by others or to stop other traders using your mark – even for different types of goods or services to those for which your mark is registered.
- It can be easier and cheaper to enforce registered trade mark rights than if you have to rely upon passing off.
- Having a registration or an application underway can enable you to protect a trade mark in circumstances where you would otherwise have no claim for passing off, such as where you have not yet traded, a business start up or new product launch.
- Can be used to prevent competitors from using your trade mark in unfair comparative advertising.
- It is easier to show potential purchasers or licensees that you own the rights that are to be sold or licensed and that they can be protected.
- Can deter other traders from adopting the same or a similar trade mark as yours.
- By registering a trade mark through the international system or as a Community trade mark, you can protect a trade mark in other countries before you have done any trading there.

Cons

- Registration and renewal fees are payable for trade mark applications (see page 86).
- In some cases you may face opposition to your application and have to fight to obtain a registration. This might happen if, for example, the owner of an existing registered trade mark felt that your proposed mark was too similar to its own mark.
- Even when registered, your trade mark registration can still be attacked either on the basis of its alleged validity or through an application for revocation.

The limitations of trade mark rights

The European Economic Area (EEA) (see page 40) is supposed to be a place where there is free movement of goods between member countries. So it is important to remember that, generally speaking, once you have placed goods bearing your trade marks on the EEA market, you cannot use those rights to stop the goods being moved across borders.

Say, for example, you sell 500 picnic bags bearing your trade mark to a wholesaler in England; he, in turn, sells them to another UK retailer. Then a buyer for a German company buys the picnic bags from the retailer and ships them to Germany for sale there. In that situation, you cannot use your trade mark rights to stop the picnic bags from being exported and sold in Germany. Those rights are 'exhausted' by the free movement of goods rule.

The position is different, however, if the goods are being imported from outside the EEA. In that scenario, you must have the permission of the ultimate trade mark owner to bring them into the EEA or the goods will be illegal for sale anywhere in the EEA.

❝Once you have placed goods bearing your trade marks on the EEA market, you cannot use those rights to stop the goods being moved across borders, because there is free movement between member countries.❞

Infringements of IP rights, including registered trade marks, are covered in Chapter 10 (pages 182–202).

Registering your trade mark

Once you have decided on a suitable trade mark that you think can be registered, you need to start the registration process as soon as possible. You can do this yourself or seek professional help.

USING A PROFESSIONAL

If you have decided that you need a trade mark registration, you should think seriously about contacting a trade mark professional to help you with the application. A professional can give you initial guidance on the suitability of your chosen trade mark and whether the mark is likely to have an easy ride through the application stages.

A professional will then draft the all-important specification that is to accompany your application so that it relates to the right kind of goods or services. He or she can also advise on the extent to which you may need more than one trade mark, such as one for the name of your business and one for its logo. Where relevant, the agent can advise you on filing for protection overseas.

The only disadvantage of using the services of a trade mark agent or other specialist is that on top of the official fees you have to pay to the registry for the registration (see page 86), you will have to pay search and professional fees for the agent's services. In practice, this can push up the cost of applying to register a trade mark significantly.

If you decide not to instruct an agent or do not have the resources to do so,

then it is perfectly possible to file for trade mark protection yourself. Inevitably, though, you need to balance what it may be costing you in terms of time dealing with the process. If you have a multitude of other things to do in getting your business off the ground, that time could be better spent more profitably on other activities (see also the pros and cons box on page 84).

FILING YOUR APPLICATION

There are only two kinds of registered trade mark that have effect in the UK: a UK trade mark registration and a registration for a Community trade mark (see pages 87–8).

A UK registration will only protect your trade mark in the UK. That is fine if you will only ever trade here but, especially in the internet age, it is possible to reach out to overseas markets, too. A failure to protect a successful trade mark in those territories can have expensive consequences (see the case study on page 84). It may lead to clashes further down the line involving litigation or re-branding. Also, if you end up wanting to sell your business, having exclusive rights in a larger territory than the UK can make the business more valuable.

Applying to register a trade mark

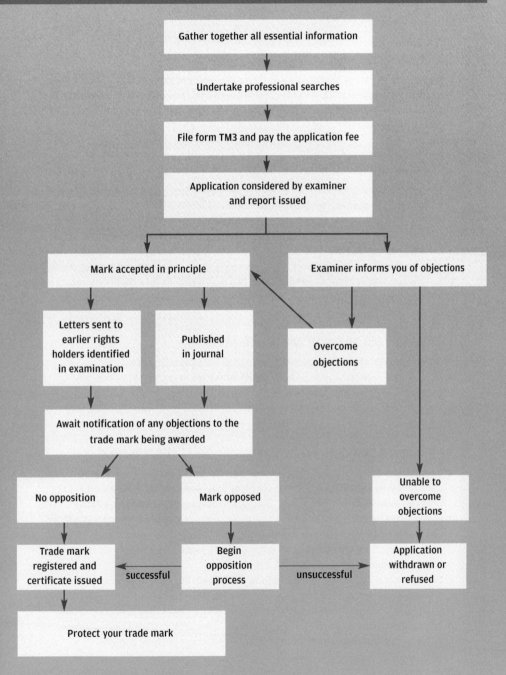

Applying for a trade mark in the UK

For an unopposed mark, the time from filing to registration in the UK can be as little as six months.

1 Gather together all essential information

- The fees you pay at registration are non-refundable so it is important that you do not make mistakes on the application. If you are applying for anything beyond a word trade mark, you need a graphic representation of the mark you are applying for. Also choose the class or classes that you want to apply for (see pages 70-3).

2 Undertake professional searches

- There is no obligation as part of the process to carry out a search first. It is merely advisory to do so. For a fee (see page 86), the IPO offers a Search and Advisory Service (SAS). Under this facility, you can ask a professional examiner at the IPO to make a search of your chosen mark in the chosen class and to provide you with a report. The report is provided within ten working days.
- In addition to the 'do it yourself' searches outlined on pages 78-9 and the IPO search, you could ask a trade mark agent or solicitor to carry out a search on your behalf. While he or she may not come up with anything in addition to the SAS report, you can then discuss the results and get appropriate advice. Trade mark agents tend not to charge substantial fees for searches.

3 File form TM3 and pay the application fee

- Fill in form TM3, which is available from the IPO website (www.ipo.gov.uk).
- You can make your application using an electronic version of the form or print it off, complete it and send with payment.
- There are also helpful guidance notes and a wealth of information on the website.

4 Application considered by examiner and report issued

- Once the application has been filed, it is examined by the IPO to see if the proposed trade mark meets the absolute requirements for registration and does not obviously offend any rules (see page 74). The IPO no longer objects to trade mark applications on 'relative grounds' (see page 75), it merely identifies them in its examination report and it is left to you to decide whether it is worth proceeding with the application in the face of those earlier marks. The IPO's examination report is usually issued within one month after filing of the application.
- If the mark is accepted in principle, it will be published in the *Trade Marks Journal* on the IPO website. Letters are also sent to any earlier right holders identified in the examination.
- If the registry raises opposition to the mark, you have the right to seek a hearing to make representations to try to overcome the objections. If that fails, there is a right of appeal, either to 'the appointed person' or to the court (see the case study on page 85).

5 Await notification of any objections to the trade mark being awarded

- From the date of publication, there is a two-month period within which anyone who wants to object to the mark can do so (see the box 'What to do if a third party files an opposition' on page 86). Many trade mark holders have opted into the IPO's notification system so that they are notified automatically by the IPO of any published trade mark applications that may clash with their own marks.
- If the registry itself does not raise objections and, after publication, no notice of opposition is filed by a third party within the three-month period, the mark can proceed to registration.

6 Protect your trade mark

- A registered trade mark can be renewed indefinitely for periods of ten years at a time. However, that is not necessarily the end of the matter. Like a house or a garden, trade mark rights must be tended and maintained (see Points to watch, pages 85–6).
- Opt in to the IPO website to be notified by the registry of any applications by third parties to register marks that are similar to yours. This enables you to ward off threats to your rights by opposing applications by others.
- The topics of trade mark infringement and how to deal with infringers is covered separately in Chapter 10.

> **"** It can take as little as six months from filing to registration to obtain an unopposed trade mark in the UK. **"**

The pros and cons of using a trade mark agent or lawyer

Pros	Cons
• Professionally qualified and can advise you – is bound to know the law and processes better than you.	• More expensive in the short term because you have to pay professional fees on top of the official fees.
• May save you time and money by steering you in the right direction earlier than if you soldiered on yourself.	
• The trade mark application could be of critical importance to the success of your business – why take the risk of going it alone?	
• Outsourcing the process to a professional frees up your time to spend elsewhere within your business.	
• The agent is unlikely to mess up your application, but if this did happen, you might be able to claim compensation from them. If you do it yourself and make a mistake – you pay for it yourself.	

Case Study   Peter

Peter has a small business in Birmingham selling organic soaps and shower gels in the Midlands under the brand name CHEVDON. The business starts to take off and he sets up a website at www.chevdon.com and applies to register a trade mark in the UK to protect his CHEVDON brand. A year later, he is approached by a distributor in Germany who is interested in taking the product and selling it in Germany. But before Peter can reach a deal with the German distributor, he learns that a rival trader has applied to register the CHEVDON trade mark in Germany, the

Benelux countries and France. The German distributor abandons plans to trade with Peter since he will be unable to use Peter's brand name in Germany without infringing the rival's trade mark registrations.

If Peter had applied for a Community trade mark from the outset, his filing would then have pre-dated the German company's attempts to file for trade mark protection. As a result, Peter would have had a platform on which to market his CHEVDON brand to the whole of Europe and not been limited by his rival's actions.

For information on finding and choosing a solicitor or trade mark agent, see pages 15-19. The website for the Institute of Trade mark Attorneys is at www.itma.org.uk.

Points to watch

After your trade mark has become registered there are still some things that you need to be aware of. Otherwise, if you are not careful you could put your trade mark at risk.

- **Registered trade marks remain open to attack** on the grounds that they are invalid and should never have been registered or that the right to the mark has been lost since registration. For example, if for a continuous period of five years after registration, you do not actually use your registered trade mark in relation to the goods or services for which it is registered, your mark becomes vulnerable. If you were to try to enforce it against anyone, they might be able to have the mark revoked for non-use.

- If you allow your trade mark to **become a common term or phrase** or allow it to be used generically, it may become similarly vulnerable. For example, the words 'escalator' and 'aspirin' were once registered trade marks, but ceased to be distinctive enough and were revoked. Where the trade mark is licensed (see pages 166–72), ensure there are strict terms in the licence to bolster the correct use of the trade mark and to avoid misuse, such as use as an ordinary word.
- **Acquiescence over a long period** in what would normally be infringement of the mark could lead to a loss of your rights.
- **Failure to oppose applications** for similar marks by other traders could lead to an erosion in the distinctiveness of the mark.

Case Study Stefan

Stefan applied to register the following slogan as a trade mark: THERE AIN'T NO F IN JUSTICE for various types of clothing. Initially, his application was objected to by the registry on the grounds that the mark was offensive. He filed evidence in writing to the IPO to answer the objections, setting out his evidence (the IPO website provides help and guidance on how to put together such a witness statement).

His application was then allowed by the registry in relation to some types of clothing, such as suits, but it was refused for use on T-shirts and baseball caps.

The registry held that if the slogan appeared on those types of goods, it would not be viewed as a trade mark (as a badge of trade origin), but rather simply as a slogan. After all, people were used to seeing slogans on caps and T-shirts.

Stefan appealed against this registry decision to 'the appointed person', a suitably qualified official, such as a barrister skilled in trade mark law, appointed by the IPO who hears appeals against decisions by registry officials. He was successful and the mark proceeded to registration.

What to do if a third party files an opposition

In some instances, it may be possible to reach an agreement with an opposing party by agreeing to amend the specification of goods or services. But if they are determined to oppose the trade mark, you have to decide whether to abandon the application or fight them.

Faced with opposition, it is advisable to seek professional advice from trade mark agents or a solicitor specialising in IP matters. If possible, you will want to try to gain an understanding of your likely prospects before you to ahead and incur the costs of resisting the opposition.

If the opposition is successful, it will stop the mark being registered. If it fails, the application process will continue.

- Once your mark is registered, use the ® symbol next to it wherever possible to denote its status (it is a criminal offence to use the ® symbol if the mark is not registered). Prior to registration, use the ™ symbol.

A WORD ABOUT COSTS

The costs of applying for trade mark protection vary according to a combination of factors. There are fixed costs (see the box below), which can be accurately predicted in advance. However, there are also items that are not predictable, such as the costs of overcoming objections raised by the trade marks registry or dealing with an opposition to the trade mark filed by a rival trader.

A single UK trade mark application for protection in one class of goods could, if unopposed, cost as little as £250 if done without professional help, or several hundred pounds more if done via a reasonably priced firm of trade mark agents. If protection is sought for multiple classes of goods and services and an application is made for a Community trade mark (see opposite), the costs would certainly be in four figures. If oppositions were raised, this would increase costs still further.

Most trade mark agents should be able to give you a good estimate of what the costs will be in advance – assuming there are no objections or oppositions to be overcome during the process.

The fixed costs of filing for a UK registered trade mark

IPO Search and Advisory Servies (SAS)	£80 plus VAT
Any additional classes to be searched	£10 plus VAT
IPO registration fee	£200
Any additional classes to apply for	£50
Renewal fee (every ten years)	£200
Renewal fee for each additional class	£50

Protection overseas

Trade marks are territorial rights so have no effect outside of the territory of registration. If, for example, you want to protect your trade mark in the US, you must register it there. Your UK trade mark registration will not prevent anyone selling goods under that trade mark in the US.

WHAT ARE THE OPTIONS?

There are three options for filing protection outside the UK:

- Community trade marks.
- International filings.
- National filings in individual countries.

Community trade marks

It is possible to file a single application for a registered trade mark known as a Community trade mark (CTM) through the Office for the Harmonisation of the Internal Market (OHIM). If this application is granted, it creates a right that applies across all 27 Member States of the EU.

CTMs are very important to businesses that are looking to market their products in other EU countries. You need to think carefully whether or not you are likely to need access to other markets in the EU beyond the UK. If you do, then if resources allow, consider applying for a CTM.

The same law applies to CTMs as to UK trade marks, so you can largely apply exactly the same legal rules and principles outlined on pages 80–6.

Applying for a CTM

The content of the application is similar to that of the UK process. Again, guidance and FAQs are available on the OHIM website to help you through the process if you are filing the application yourself, rather than using a trade mark agent.

- The application for a CTM can be made online via the OHIM website.
- The initial filing fee for a CTM is €750. A further fee of €850 is payable on registration. This includes registration for the mark in up to three different classes of goods or services. Additional fees of €150 are payable for each additional class.

For more information on applying for Community trade mark registration, visit the OHIM website at http://oami.europa.eu.

Inevitably, with the application covering 27 countries, there is a greater chance of opposition to a CTM application than with a national application. However, if it becomes clear that there are too many oppositions for the mark to make it as a CTM, the application can be turned into a set of national trade mark applications in those countries where there is unlikely to be such a problem.

In such a case, the filing date of the CTM application will count as the priority filing date for the national applications.

International filings

If you want to register your trade mark in a number of countries outside the EU, then go through the World International Property Organisation (WIPO). Registering in this way enables a single application to be made for trade marks in a number of countries simultaneously. However, the applications are treated as national filings by the relevant trade marks registry for each country concerned and the national law of that country will apply. The fees are payable in Swiss Francs and are variable.

It can be very difficult to keep abreast of such filings overseas, so it is strongly recommended that you instruct a trade mark agent to deal with such applications. They are likely to have contacts in other jurisdictions and can ensure that the process is administered cost effectively and more cheaply than if you had to approach local agents directly.

" Registering through WIPO enables a single application to be made for trade marks in a number of countries. "

For more information on international trade mark applications via WIPO visit www.wipo.int/trade marks/en/.

Design protection

Designs are a type of IP right that all businesses should be aware of - and increasingly so. Prior to 6 March 2002, design protection was largely restricted to three-dimensional objects and articles. But new design laws from Europe changed all that. As a result, the scope of what can now be protected under design law has become far wider, so businesses must consider design protection issues.

The value of design protection

Like other IP rights, rights in designs can give your business a competitive advantage by preventing trading rivals from exploiting designs you have originated. Another advantage of design protection is that achieving it through registration is cheaper and more straightforward than for other IP rights, such as patents and trade marks.

If you own a protected design, you can potentially stop anyone from using, importing, selling or making anything that incorporates your design or a design very similar to it. By controlling the rights to the design (potentially for up to 25 years), you may be able to create an income stream through licensing it to others, or command higher prices for goods sold based on the design.

That said, not every business will need to prioritise the protection of its designs over other types of IP rights. But in order to understand better whether design

protection is relevant and necessary, it is essential to understand some of the basics of how design laws work. The focus of this chapter is on the main types of design law that are encountered in the UK, namely those derived from EU laws.

DESIGN LAW BASICS

The main design laws applying to the UK provide protection for the appearance of the whole or a part of 'products' resulting from the features of, in particular, their lines, contours, colours, shape, textures, materials or ornamentation.

For these purposes, 'product' means any industrial or handicraft item other than a computer program and includes packaging, '**get up**', graphic symbols, typographic typefaces and parts intended to be assembled into a **complex product**.

The scope of what can be protected is potentially very large indeed. Just how large can be illustrated by the following list of examples of designs protected by current design laws:

- An air freshener canister.
- Alloy wheels.

Jargon buster

Complex product A product consisting of at least two replaceable component parts permitting product disassembly or reassembly

'Get up' A description of how a product looks in its packaging. For example, the 'get up' of a Jif lemon is the yellow lemon-shaped container that the Jif lemon juice comes in

- The emblem of a football club.
- A female hygiene product.
- A handbag.
- A crispy snack.
- The head of a golf club.
- A pattern for a carpet.
- A company logo.
- A shoe tread pattern.
- A shower fixing.
- The mesh of a fishing bait container.

The list is truly endless!

It is important to appreciate, however, that modern design protection is concerned with the design itself rather than the type of product to which the design is initially applied. So, for example, if a design is registered for the appearance of a new model of telephone, that design right would still enable the design owner to prevent someone using the same design as a novelty pencil sharpener or cigarette lighter in the shape of that telephone.

The new design laws

The revamping of design laws in 2002 has not only increased the scope of designs that can be protected, but there are two further aspects of the design regime that are worth noting:

- **Registering designs is now relatively cheap and straightforward.** Unlike patents and, to an extent registered trade marks, filing a design application does not invariably require the involvement of expensive professional fees or large filing costs. Anyone can do it with appropriate care (see pages 97–104).
- **The creation of a Community design** has made it possible for businesses to acquire protection for designs across 27 EU states by means of just one application. This is very useful for businesses that may want to trade in other European markets (see pages 105–6).

Designs that cannot have design protection

There are exceptions to design protection. The most important of these are:

- Where the appearance of the design is dictated solely by its technical function (this does not, however, apply to UK unregistered design (see pages 107-8).
- The design consists of features that must be adopted so the product fits or connects to another product.
- The design is contrary to public policy, such as a design for the appearance of a handgun disguised as an everyday object.
- The design would involve the improper use of certain emblems, such as the Royal coat of arms.
- The design conflicts with an earlier application for protection or another IP right.

Seek design protection whenever possible

There is some overlap between copyright law and the law of designs. Also, it is possible to register trade marks for shapes, the appearance of packaging, logos and other items that can also be protected as designs. But there are reasons why it can sometimes be unwise to rely on trade marks or copyright. These involve some complex legal issues, which are beyond the scope of this book.

Suffice to say that, particularly where a shape of something is concerned, you would be wise to seek design protection for that shape as well, rather than relying solely on a trade mark registration. The law concerning shape marks is in an uncertain state so the risk of relying on a trade mark to protect a shape is that it might end up being declared invalid leaving you with no protection. Since you cannot register a design after 12 months have elapsed from when you first made the design public, if you don't register the design early on, it might be too late to go and get one later.

TYPES OF DESIGN PROTECTION

There are four types of design protection available in the UK. These are:

- Community registered designs.
- Community unregistered designs.
- UK registered designs.
- UK unregistered designs.

Fortunately, due to EU harmonisation laws, much of the law relating to the first three now overlaps substantially. It is really the fourth kind – UK unregistered design – that is the odd one out. These days, UK unregistered design protection tends to be less important in practice than the others, and is covered on pages 107–8.

❝ Unregistered designs are rights that acquire protection without any formal process. ❞

Registered versus unregistered designs

As their description suggests, registered designs are rights that are protected through registration. Unregistered designs are rights that, like copyright, acquire automatic protection without any formal process – provided they meet certain requirements.

There is another important difference between registered and unregistered design rights. Registered designs confer on the design owner a complete monopoly over the particular design in question. In other words, for as long as the design protection is in place, no one else is able to use the protected design or one very similar to it – even if they arrived at their design independently.

Unregistered designs, by contrast, only protect against the copying of the design by others. So, if someone comes up with a design that is very similar to an existing unregistered design, but didn't get there by copying, there is nothing the owner of the unregistered design can do about it.

Why register?

Given that unregistered design protection applies automatically to new designs, assuming they meet the criteria for design protection (see overleaf), why should anyone bother to register their designs? There are, in fact, a number of advantages to registering a design over relying solely on unregistered rights – see the box below.

The pros and cons of registering a design

Pros	Cons
• Registered designs can be made to last up to 25 years from the date on which you first revealed the design to the public. Community unregistered designs last for only three years and UK unregistered designs for only ten years from that date. So registration gives you a significantly longer period of protection for your design.	• Filing fees have to be paid to the appropriate registry for each registration. However, the fees are relatively modest (£60 for a UK registration) (see page 98) and for Community filings, the unit cost of each design application is reduced substantially for multiple applications.
• Registered designs give you a monopoly on the use of that design (in relation to any product that embodies the design). Unregistered design rights only protect against copying.	• Registration does not prevent another party from challenging the validity of the protected design on the grounds that it did not meet the requirements for protection at the time of registration. This may increase the expense of enforcing the design against infringers.
• Enforcement of suspected infringements of registered designs is much more straightforward – and potentially much cheaper – than enforcing unregistered design rights (see pages 107-8).	
• If a design is registered, this is likely to afford you a commercial advantage when selling a business or licensing the rights in the design. It adds value to have the registration as a visible asset of the business.	
• Having a design registered may help to discourage rivals from adopting designs that are too similar to the protected design. Competitors can search the register of designs to check for clashes. They cannot do that for unregistered designs.	

THE CHIEF REQUIREMENTS FOR DESIGN PROTECTION

Leaving aside UK unregistered designs for a moment, in order to acquire protection, a design needs to meet the following key criteria when compared with designs made available to the public before the 'relevant date'.

- **It must be 'new'**, which means that it must not be identical, except for immaterial, minor details when compared to any relevant prior design that has already been made available to the public.
- **It must have 'individual character'**, which means that the new design must create a 'different overall impression' on the **informed user** when compared to **prior art**.

Jargon buster

Informed user A fictional person through whose eyes the court judges whether a design has individual character. The informed user is not an expert in the relevant field, but nor is he or she an ordinary consumer. Rather the informed user is a person in between those extremes who is familiar with designs in the sector concerned

Prior Art (design) The pre-existing designs against which the validity of a protected design is assessed to see if it really is 'new' or has 'individual character'

Grace period

Where there is a registered design, any disclosure made by the designer or his or her agent in relation to the design during the 12 months preceding the application for registration is ignored. So if you want to register your design, you have a 'grace period' after revealing the design within which you can test the market before incurring any registration fees. But there are dangers in doing this as is illustrated by the case study opposite.

❝ To be registered, a design must meet key criteria. ❞

The 'relevant date'

The 'relevant date' at which you judge whether a design is 'new' or has 'individual character' is set as follows:

- **For registered designs**: the date on which an application to register the design is filed (or where a priority date is claimed – the date of priority).
- **For unregistered designs**: the date on which the design has first been made available to the public.

A design is treated as having been 'made available to the public' once it has been published following registration or otherwise. This is also the case once it has been exhibited, used in trade or otherwise disclosed (except where the designer has disclosed the design confidentially).

But it will not be treated as having been made available to the public if any such events could not reasonably have become known in the normal course of business to the circles specialised in the sector concerned, operating in the EU.

> **❝ It pays to register immediately where a product may have a long selling life, but not for fashion items with a short saleable period. ❞**

Case Study Carl

Carl is a designer who sets up in business with Emily, an accountant. In February, Carl created a new design for a stylish and original table lamp. He wanted to register a Community design for his new creation, but Emily wanted to see if any interested parties could be found to market the new design before incurring the filing fees for registering the design. She relied on the 12-month grace period (see box, opposite), confident that in the interim anyone who copied Carl's design during that period would have infringed the business's unregistered design rights.

A few months later, after some hard selling, Carl's design is very well received by the market and is clearly going to be successful. So in August, Emily agrees they should now file for registration. But disaster! It turns out that in June, a designer in Italy who knew nothing about Carl and Emily's business, happens to have created a very similar design and has filed an application to register it as a Community design.

Carl and Emily may be able to oppose the Italian designer's application to register its design on the basis that it is not 'new' or does not have 'individual character' compared to Carl's earlier design. However, the existence of the Italian design will also now block them from obtaining a registration for their own design. This is because, at the date they file their own application, Carl's design will no longer be 'new' or have 'individual character' compared to previous designs – the Italian design.

Carl and Emily will now have only three years protection as a Community unregistered design and up to ten years protection as a UK unregistered design, and they have lost out on the chance of monopolising a lucrative design for the next 25 years.

So the moral is, unless you really cannot afford it, where the product is something that may have a long selling life, it pays to register immediately. The position might be different with, for example, fashion items like clothes, the designs for which may only be saleable for a year or two before they go out of fashion.

95

OWNERSHIP OF DESIGNS

As with any form of IP protection, you must be careful that the ownership of title to the design resides with the right person.

Generally, the designer is the first owner of title to the design. Similarly, as a general rule, if the designer is an employee who creates the design in the course of his or her employment, title to the design will vest in the employer.

Difficulties may occur where the relationship between the business owner and the designer is not so clear cut and they aren't one and the same person.

Under UK design law, if you commission a third party in return for payment to create the design for you, then title to the design will vest in you as commissioner – not the designer. But, confusingly, there is no such rule with Community designs.

So if you use the services of a third party to create something for you and you want title to the Community design protection, you must make sure that a term to that effect is in your contract with the designer.

❝ If the designer is someone who creates the design as part of his or her employment, title to the design will vest in the employer. ❞

Registering for protection

There are a number of advantages to having a design registered rather than trusting to unregistered design protection. If you decide to register a design or designs, the route you take (and the associated costs) will depend on whether or not you want protection for your design to extend beyond the UK.

REGISTERING IN THE UK VERSUS OVERSEAS

If you want only protection within the UK, you need only apply to register the design here in the UK (see overleaf). This would be the cheapest form of registration. But it would also give you the narrowest protection.

If you want to protect your design in other countries, you will have to make some choices. These would be:

- **To apply for a Community design registration.** This would, if granted, protect your design in all 27 Member States of the EU (including, of course, the UK).
- **To apply for an international registration.** You would do this through the World Intellectual Property Organisation (WIPO), a body based in Switzerland that operates a centralised system for protecting trade marks and designs on an international basis.
- **If there are specific countries where you want protection,** you could make national filings for protection at the national design registry of each country concerned.

In practice, it is unlikely that you would want to take the third option because it is much easier to use the Community design or WIPO systems than making separate national applications.

❝ There are a number of options for protecting your design in countries other than the UK. ❞

 Information for Community design protection is given on pages 105-6, and that for national registration is on page 106.

Getting professional help

In an ideal world, it would always be preferable to engage the services of a professional in advising you and helping you with the process of registering your designs. However, compared with trade marks and patents, the process of applying to register a design is much less complicated and protracted. If money is tight, you are likely to be better off using professionals, if possible, to help with your trade mark and/or patent filings and dealing with the designs yourself.

Before coming to a decision, think carefully about your plans and objectives for your business. Clearly, having monopoly protection for your design across multiple countries will be potentially more valuable in the long term to your business. But will the extra costs be worth it (see below and page 105)?

" If money is tight, you could register a design yourself as the process is less complicated. "

The fixed costs of filing for a UK registered design

1st application	£60
Subsequent designs as part of a multiple application[a]	£40
Renewal fees	
For years 6-10	£130
For years 11-15	£210
For years 16-20	£310
For years 21-25	£450

a Where you apply to register more than one design at once. You might also want to file multiple applications of the same design so you cover various combinations, such as one application for the whole of the design, another for a part of it and so on.

 Copies of the relevant forms for UK registration are available online from the IPO website at www.ipo.gov.org. IPO also publish helpful booklets explaining how to complete the forms.

The UK registered design process

An unobjectionable UK application will usually take three to four months from the date of filing to the date of registration. The diagram below summarises the application process and more detailed information is given overleaf.

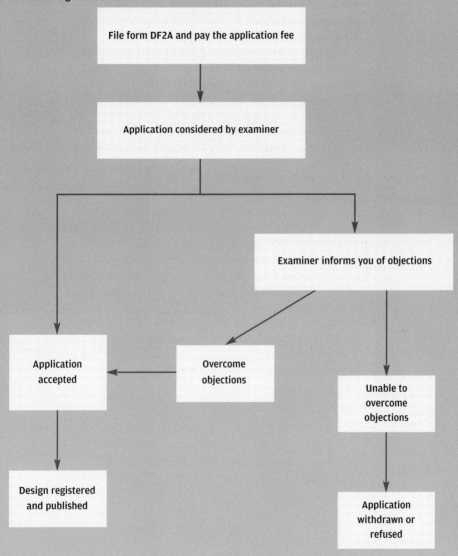

File form DF2A and pay the application fee

Application considered by examiner

Examiner informs you of objections

Application accepted

Overcome objections

Unable to overcome objections

Design registered and published

Application withdrawn or refused

1   File form DF2A and pay the application fee

- The form and an explanatory booklet are available from the IPO website (www.ipo.gov.uk). To complete the form you will need the following information:
  - The name and address of the applicant (the person or business who is to be the owner of the design).
  - The type of product the design has been created for (or if it is decoration, the type of product that it could be applied to; or if a shape, the kind of product it could be used for).
  - Clear illustrations of the design – whether in the form of drawings or photographs (including different views of the design).
  - If your design is a pattern, you must show the complete pattern and repeats of the pattern so the repeat is also protected.
  - Unless obvious from the illustration, you may need a few descriptive words to explain any features of the design that are not obvious from looking at the illustration or photograph.
  - If you are only seeking design protection for a part of the product shown in the illustration, you need to make that clear – either in the illustration itself or by a suitable description, or via both means.
  - If you want to defer publication and registration of the design, you need to indicate this on the form where required.
  - If you are claiming priority from an earlier design application filed in another country, you must provide details.

“ All forms and explanatory booklets are available from the IPO website. ”

2   The application is considered by the examiner

- The IPO ensures the form has been correctly filled in and the fee paid. The office also checks that the design is not dictated solely by how the product works, that it isn't offensive and that it doesn't use protected emblems.
- It does not examine questions of whether the design is new or has individual character, which means the criteria can only be enforced in retrospect. It is up to anyone who objects to the design after it is registered to file invalidity proceedings (or, if they are sued by the design owner, to file a counterclaim for invalidity in those proceedings) (see the case studies on page 104).

3   IPO notifies you of acceptance or of any objections

- If satisfied, the IPO will write to you (usually within two months of receiving the application) and confirm the application is accepted or explain the objections. If accepted, details of the design are then published by the IPO on their website, and is put on the register.
- If there are objections, you can ask for a hearing so that you can try to overcome the objections (see the case study on page 85).

“The IPO does not look into whether the design is new or has individual character.”

RENEWAL FEES

You have to renew your registration periodically to keep it in force. This helps with flexibility. If a trade mark or a design ceases to be of any use or, for example, if the owner goes out of business, the registration will lapse. There is no point in deterring people from using something that is no longer in use.

The fees increase over time because it is assumed that in the early days the owner might be short of cash, whereas it is assumed that if you still want your design to be kept on the register ten years later, you are using it commercially and making money from it. The renewal fees are paid to the IPO in the case of UK registered designs or to the Office for the Harmonisation of the Internal Market (OHIM) for Community designs.

❝ You have to renew your registration periodically to keep it in force, and the fees will increase over time, too. ❞

TIPS FOR A SUCCESSFUL DESIGN REGISTRATION

Remember that just because you manage to successfully register a design does not mean that you are home and dry. The validity of that design can always be challenged later on by a third party. This may happen if you try to enforce it against someone. A weak design is useless, so before undertaking the registration process, try to ensure that your design is going to stand up and be resistant to any attack. How can you do this?

- **Understand the essentials of how design law works** and, in particular, what is meant by the requirement that the design be 'new' and have 'individual character' (see page 94). Do not be put off if you do not understand it all at first – lawyers have similar difficulties!

- **Make some design searches** before you publicise your design or file an application to register it, to see if there is anything similar to your design that has already been filed. This will give you an opportunity to make changes to your design to try to avoid overlap with what is already there. You may alternatively find that your design is too similar to the prior art (see below). Bear in mind that it isn't that easy to make a watertight design search. As at December 2008, you can make design searches on the IPO site and also OHIM's site, searching by product type. Another rough and ready search is to use Google images. For example, if you have designed a table lamp you could search for pictures of table lamps and scroll through the results (although for something like that you could also search websites of people who sell table lamps).

- **Make sure that in your application you clearly identify what the design is** and, where appropriate, show the design from different perspectives.

- **Focus on the essentials of the design.** If its scope is too wide, it will be easier for it to be challenged on the grounds that it is not new or does not have individual character compared to similar prior designs.

Prior art

Registered designs are not subjected to much in the way of scrutiny by the appropriate registration office at the application stage, so there is little or no assessment of whether they really meet the relevant requirements for design protection. It is often the case, therefore, that when confronted by a design claim, the party under attack will try to find evidence to challenge the validity of the design.

In the case of a registered design, the design is treated as valid unless the contrary is proved. In the case of an unregistered design the party claiming the right will need to support its claim to have protection by showing how and when the design was created.

To successfully challenge the validity of a design and 'knock out' any claim based on that design, the defendant needs to demonstrate that the protected design falls foul of one or more of the statutory requirements for design protection. Most commonly, this will involve an attack on the novelty or individual character of the design.

The party challenging the design right will try to convince the court that the protected design is too similar to a previous design (known as 'the prior art'). If the court is persuaded that in

❝ It is often the case that when confronted by a design claim, the party under attack will try to find evidence to challenge the validity of the design relied on in the claim. ❞

comparison to that earlier design(s), the protected design is identical or does not have sufficient 'individual character', it will declare the protected design to be invalid. This will strip it of all effect.

The scope of the 'prior art' that can be relied on in this way to invalidate a design is narrower than the prior art used in patent cases. A UK patent, for example, can be invalidated for lack of novelty if there is anything at all by way of relevant prior art anywhere in the world. It does not matter whether or not that prior art could reasonably have been known about by anyone in the UK at the time.

In design cases, however, the prior art is more restricted. It only extends to prior designs that could reasonably have been known to people carrying on business in the EEA specialising in the sector concerned. The 'sector concerned' for these purposes is the sector of the prior art − not the sector covered by the product to which the protected design has been applied.

The application of these provisions is illustrated by the two case studies set out overleaf.

Case Study | Chris

Chris obtains protection from 1 January 2007 for a registered design for a spiky ball that is to be used as a plaything for pet dogs.

In June 2007, Chris's competitor, David, produces a similar spiky ball for dogs. Chris objects and sues David for infringing his design. In his defence, David attacks the validity of Chris's design on the basis that he can show that in 2005, an identical spiky ball design was being sold on the internet for use as a massage aid. David proves that design circles in the EU specialising in the health products sector would have been aware of the prior design for the spiky massage ball before 1 January 2007 – before the date from which Chris's design took effect.

Chris's design is therefore declared invalid and the effect is that it will be as if the design was never registered in the first place. His design was not 'new' at the relevant time and so does not meet the requirements for protection as a registered design.

Case Study | Jean

In the spring of 2008, Jean creates a design for a metallic CD holder. She has it manufactured in Taiwan and imported for sale in the UK in time for Christmas. Copycat Ltd, a UK furniture manufacturer, sees the design on sale. Copycat asks its manufacturer in India to copy the design so that Copycat can import and sell the CD holder in the UK. Jean discovers the Copycat product on sale and sues Copycat for design infringement. Copycat asks its Indian supplier to help it research some prior art with which to attack the validity of Jean's design. The Indians discover by chance that a local shop in the capital of South Korea has been selling a very similar design of CD holder for five years previously.

Copycat asks the English court to rule that Jean's design is invalid because it does not have 'individual character' compared to the Korean shop's prior design. The court rejects Copycat's argument. Although it accepts that Jean's design does not create a different overall impression on the informed user compared to the Korean design, it finds that the Korean design was only on sale locally in one shop in Seoul.

Accordingly, the Korean design could not 'reasonably have been known to design circles in the EU' specialising in the design of hi fi accessories, at the time Jean's design was first made public. Copycat's challenge to the validity of Jean's design fails.

APPLYING FOR COMMUNITY DESIGN PROTECTION

A Community design registration will protect your design in all 27 Member States of the EU (including the UK). It can also be used as a priority filing, so giving rise to your priority date if you want to seek protection in non-EU countries as well. The law governing what can and can't qualify for design protection is the same for a Community registered design as it is for a UK registered design.

The application procedure is also very similar to that for a UK registered design. You will need to provide essentially the same information, including illustrations of your design. The application can be filed with the IPO, who will pass it on to the Office for the Harmonisation of the Internal Market (OHIM), the official EU agency that administers Community designs and Community trade marks,

The cost of filing for a Community registered design

The fees for registering a Community design are more expensive than for UK registered designs (although they do, of course, cover a much larger territory). However, renewal fees are much cheaper. The table below shows the discounts available for multiple design applications. For example, if five applications are filed, the fee payable would be: 350 + (175 x 4) = €1,050

No of applications	Filing fee (€)		Publication fee (€)[a]		Total fee per application (€)
1st	230	+	120	=	350
2nd-10th	115	+	60	=	175
11th +	50	+	30	=	80
Renewal fees					
For years 6-10			€90		
For years 11-15			€120		
For years 16-20			€150		
For years 21-25			€180		

a Should you want to delay publication, you can pay a deferment fee, which is currently €60, which you pay instead of the publication fee. The publication fee must be paid in order for the application to progress.

For more information on registering for Community design registration, visit the OHIM website at http://oami.europa.eu.

based in Alicante, Spain. Or it can be filed directly to at OHIM. OHIM also has a facility for direct filing over the internet via its website, together with full notes and FAQs on how to do this.

Timescales

There is no opposition procedure for Community designs and no detailed examination of applications, so applications should be processed within a few months.

APPLYING FOR INTERNATIONAL REGISTRATION

An alternative to filing through OHIM is to take advantage of the fact that since 1 January 2008, the EU has joined the international treaty on industrial designs. This means that it is now possible for design owners to file applications for protection in multiple countries, including the EU, with WIPO.

A registered design filed with WIPO can, if granted, be enforceable as a Community design in exactly the same way as if it had been filed with OHIM.

Like OHIM, WIPO has its own facility for direct filing of applications over the internet. Detailed rules and guidance notes for how to do this appear on the WIPO website.

For information on WIPO filings visit http://www.wipo.int/export/sites/www/standards/en/pdf/03-03-01.pdf

UK unregistered design

UK unregistered design is another form of design protection, which exists independently of the other design laws. This is because UK unregistered design is governed by a separate piece of legislation, although it usually overlaps with those other laws.

The legislation gives the design owner the exclusive right to reproduce the design for commercial purposes by making articles featuring that design or making a design document recording the design for the purpose of enabling such articles to be made. It also protects against the importation, sale, stocking for sale or hire of 'infringing articles' where the person concerned knows or has reason to believe the articles infringe the design.

In most cases, UK unregistered design protection will add nothing to the protection afforded by a registered design. However, it is worth noting the following about UK unregistered designs:

- Unlike UK registered designs and Community designs, they can protect designs that are the result of a product's functional characteristics.
- The term of protection can last for a maximum of 15 years from the end of the year in which the design was first recorded in a **design document** or ten years from the date on which the design was first put to commercial use. This is significantly longer than the period of protection enjoyed by

Jargon buster

Design document A document embodying the design, such as a picture of how a film prop should look or a design drawing showing the appearance and dimensions of a design for a car

unregistered Community designs (three years), but much shorter than that of registered designs (25 years).

CRITERIA FOR PROTECTION

UK unregistered designs are created by the Copyright Designs & Patents Act 1988, the same legislation that governs copyright law. The key features of UK unregistered designs are as follows:

- They only protect the design of aspects of the 'shape and configuration' of an article or a part of an article – excluding surface decoration. So the scope of what they protect is considerably narrower than Community designs and UK registered designs.

Case Study | Jones Ltd

In 2004, Jones Ltd, a manufacturer of audio equipment, commissions an Italian designer to design an attractive new loudspeaker with an unusual shape. Having commissioned the design, Jones is the first owner of the UK unregistered design right in the new speaker design. It starts selling the new speaker in time for Christmas 2004. Jones Ltd does not apply to register the design.

In 2008, Jones notices that Ripoff & Co is selling very similar speakers in the UK at much lower prices. Jones wants to take action. However, although Jones did have Community unregistered design protection for the speaker design when it was first made available to the public, that right expired in 2007 because it only lasted three years.

Nevertheless, Jones is able to fall back on UK unregistered design protection for the new speaker, which will be in force for ten years until 2014. Of course, had Jones registered the design, the company would have had monopoly on the design for 25 years until 2029.

- Designs must be 'original' and must not be commonplace in the design field in question at the time of their creation. This differs to the rules applying to other design laws as these are subject to the novelty and individual character criteria referred to on page 94.

- They cannot protect a method or principle of construction or features that enable an article to be connected to another article so that either can perform its function; for example, a spare part for something that has to have a certain shape.

Finance

Obtaining adequate IP rights protection can, in some cases, be protracted and expensive. Sometimes these and other costs, such as those incurred in developing the product, will be too much for the inventor or budding entrepreneur to bear alone. This chapter examines other options available for financing such costs and explains what they entail and how to secure finance.

Setting up a business

One of the first decisions you need to make when setting up a business is to decide what corporate 'vehicle' you should use to take forward your invention or business. Are you going to form a company for this purpose? Or are you going to remain a sole trader?

YOUR OPTIONS

There are a number of different ways you can operate a business and own or register IP and other assets.

Sole trader

To operate as a sole trader requires no formalities and, as its name suggests, simply means you run the business under your own or a trading name. Any property or assets are owned in your name.

A sole trader pays Income Tax and (where applicable) Capital Gains Tax in the same way an individual does via the self-assessment system.

Limited company

The most common type of company that can be incorporated in the UK is a company limited by shares – more commonly referred to as a 'limited company'. A limited company is established by registering it with the registrar of companies. In England and Wales, the system is administered by Companies House in Cardiff. For companies that have their registered offices in Scotland, the relevant Companies House office is based in Edinburgh. As far as companies in Northern Ireland are concerned, these are currently administered by the companies registry in Belfast, but from 1 October 2009, that will be integrated with Companies House in England and Wales.

A limited company is formed by the **subscribers**, who agree to take shares in it and agree to its constitution, known as the Memorandum and Articles of Association. Companies also need to have a **company secretary** and at least one **director**. Companies pay **Corporation Tax** on their profits. Where they distribute profits to **shareholders** in the form of **dividends**, the recipients of the dividends pay Income Tax on those receipts.

A limited company is a 'legal person' in its own right – it can sue or be sued in its own name; it can also be prosecuted and it can own property just like an individual person can. However, if a company goes bust, then the subscribers, shareholders and directors have only **limited liability** for its debts and liabilities. So a company may be a good way of protecting yourself against business failure. However, in practice, for many small businesses, this benefit can be more illusory than real. This is because many start-ups and entrepreneurs can

Jargon buster

Company secretary An officer of a company who is responsible for maintaining statutory books and records

Corporation Tax The tax paid by companies on company profits

Directors Officers of a company – usually employees – who have special status. They not only exercise certain powers conferred on them by the company's constitution to run the affairs of the company, but they have duties and responsibilities imposed on them by company law. All companies have to have at least one director

Dividends Payments made by a company to its shareholders. Usually they are linked to a company's profits; the more profit a company makes, the higher the dividend payments it makes

Limited liability In the context of a limited company, limited liability means that if a company becomes insolvent, its liability to any creditors is limited to the value of its issued share capital

Shareholders Companies are owned by shareholders. They take shares in a company which rise or fall in value depending on the value of the company itself. They ultimately control the company and may receive dividend payments

Subscribers When a new company is formed, the persons who become its first shareholders are known as 'subscribers'

only secure financial support for their companies by giving personal guarantees to banks or landlords. The guarantees are called upon if the company fails. A limited company will often only be able to raise funds without such guarantees once it grows in value and establishes a trading track record.

The details and formalities associated with the incorporation and running of limited companies are beyond the scope of this book. However, a limited company can be 'bought off the shelf' very cheaply either directly from Companies House or from a company formation agent (the filing fee for incorporation is £20, or £50 for a same-day service), and incorporating one from scratch is straightforward.

Once you have a company, you are required to meet certain formalities in terms of filing documents with Companies House. It is important that you acquaint yourself with these rules since a failure to comply can lead to criminal sanctions and disqualification as a company director.

For more information about limited companies and incorporating them, see the Companies House website at www.companieshouse.org.uk. See also the *Which? Essential Guide* to *Working for Yourself* for more information about all types of businesses.

111

Partnership

This is an entity where at least two people carry on the business as partners with a view to making a profit. Partnerships do not need to be registered at Companies House and – unlike companies – can keep their financial affairs out of the public domain.

The partners share the profits and pay Income Tax and Capital Gains Tax in a similar way to sole traders. They also bear the business's losses and (unlike the directors of a limited company) there is no limit to the liabilities and debts of the partnership. So if a partnership fails, it may spell ruin for the partners – regardless of whether or not they have done anything wrong.

A limited liability partnership (LLP) is another type of corporate entity that sits mid way between a limited company and a partnership. An LLP has members rather than partners but pays Income Tax on the profits it makes rather than Corporation Tax. An LLP (unlike a partnership) must file its accounts at Companies House, which are available for public inspection. The advantage of an LLP over a partnership is that, as its name suggests, an LLP has limited liability up to the amount of capital invested by its members. With a partnership, the individual partners are potentially liable without limit for the debts of the partnership. So a partnership is a more risky form of business structure.

❝ There is no limit to the liabilities and debts of a partnership. If it fails, the partners could be ruined, whether or not they have done anything wrong. ❞

DECIDING WHICH TO GO FOR

There are a number of pros and cons associated with each type of vehicle, such as tax considerations and running costs. Seek appropriate professional advice, preferably from an accountant. There is no 'one solution fits all' – see also the pros and cons of setting up different business vehicles, opposite.

For more information about setting up a business, go to the following websites: www.businessbricks.co.uk, www.businessclub365.com, www.smallbusiness.co.uk, www.smallbusinessadvice.org.uk and www.ukbusinessforums.co.uk.

The pros and cons of setting up different business vehicles

Sole trader

Pros	Cons
• Few formalities required, such as the need to file accounts and documents with Companies House. • No formation fees to pay.	• Personal liability for the debts of the business if it fails. • Limited sources of finance.

Limited company

Pros	Cons
• Limited liability in case the business fails. • Increases scope for different forms of financing, such as through issuing shares. • Corporate structure suits many businesses better than other forms of business structure.	• Incorporation costs and ongoing requirement to file documents at Companies House, such as an annual return. • Financial performance has to be made public through compulsory filing of accounts.

Partnership

Pros	Cons
• No need to disclose in public details of financial performance or profits earned by the partners. • Complex companies legislation and regulatory regime does not apply, so easier for the partners to regulate their dealings.	• Partners have personal, unlimited liability for partnership debts.

Financing your idea

Whatever your invention or business idea, you will need money to finance the costs that will be incurred in exploiting it. Plan first, then look into your options for obtaining finance.

FINANCIAL PLANNING

When it comes to protecting your IP rights, be it filing for patent, design or trade mark protection, you can make an assessment of the likely costs at the outset. As is explained in the relevant chapters dealing with these rights, there are fixed fees, which you can budget for.

The fees of professional advisers are more fluid but can, nevertheless, generally be estimated with reasonable accuracy if you talk to them and ask for estimates or quotes. What is more difficult is judging the extent to which unforeseen issues and costs will arise during the registration process. There may be oppositions or objections to

" Allow for potential extra costs caused by any oppositions or objections to your applications. "

your applications, which can push up the costs. So when making your budget you need to allow for these contingencies. You may also need to cover your own living expenses if you are not working or drawing another income.

Product development

Where you are developing a product, it is likely that you will need to pay for the production of a prototype and quite possibly its testing and the costs of improving and developing it. If you are setting up, say, a website, you will have web designers to pay.

Launching your product or service

When you are ready to launch your product or service onto the market, you will need a budget to do that, too, whether it be to buy stock, marketing materials or pay for advertising. How much you will need depends on whether you have appointed a distributor or

The potential cost of registering for a patent is given on page 38, that for trade mark protection is on page 86, and design registration is given on page 98.

licensee or adopted franchising as a way of doing business.

All these costs and expenses will need to be factored into your business plan (see pages 123–4).

OBTAINING FINANCE THROUGH A LOAN

Borrowing money is something that most, if not all, businesses have to do at some point. To effect a loan, you need to find a person or another business to lend you a sum of money, which will be repaid either by instalments or at the end of a defined period. The cost of the loan is the interest that is payable on it and/or any fees that the lender also charges.

Borrowing from friends and family

This might be your first port of call. Even if a loan is taken on favourable terms from that kind of source, it is advisable to draw up some kind of written loan document to record the relevant terms. Even a very basic agreement is better than nothing.

Whoever makes you the loan, from the lender's point of view they ought to have something that shows they aren't making a gift to you and that the money is expected to be repaid (with or without interest). From the borrower's point of view, it needs to be made clear that the

loan doesn't mean any watering down of the owner's rights in the invention or IP rights in question – unless that is part of the deal.

❝When taking a loan from friends or family, even a very basic agreement is better than nothing for both the lender and the borrower.❞

Borrowing from a bank or other financial institution

Three main types of borrowing are potentially available from this source.

An overdraft facility Where you have established a business banking account, the business may have an agreed overdraft facility, in much the same way as an individual may have with his or her private bank account. Overdrafts have the advantage of flexibility in that you only borrow what you need to at any one time. But overdraft finance tends to be more expensive than other types of loan.

 To find examples of suitably worded precedents for agreements that you can download for a modest fee, go to www.clickdocs.co.uk.

115

Also, if possible, avoid taking out an unauthorised overdraft since charges and interest levied by the bank tend to be very high if you go beyond your agreed borrowing limits.

Overdrafts can also be withdrawn at very short notice by the lender, so you need to be careful not to place too much reliance on them. Your business could be ruined by the bank making a decision that you are powerless to stop.

Unsecured or secured loan Short, medium or long-term unsecured loans may be available. But it is unlikely that a bank would want to lend to a limited company or start-up business without some kind of guarantee or security. The interest rates and payment terms of such loans can be the subject of negotiation with the bank and shopping around at different places may enable you to obtain a better deal.

Secured loans (like mortgages) are another option and tend to have the lowest interest rates. If you have spare equity in your house, you may be able to raise a second mortgage. Or if you

Full time or part time?

If you are starting a business or working on an invention that you hope one day to make money from, you may find it difficult to devote enough time and attention to your project and still carry on your job at the same time.

But the fact is that you will need to pay for your outgoings, so having some form of income is obviously important, particularly as your investment in a new business venture may not show an initial return. When it comes to raising money to finance your business, most investors will not be keen to invest money in the early stages of a business if they perceive that much of their investment is simply being used to fund the income and lifestyle of the business owner. They want their money working for them in the business, not going to pay the owner's mortgage.

However, be aware that if you are an employee or a partner in a company or firm and you spend too much of your work time on your own project, you may not only be in breach of your contract, but in some situations, your employer or firm might be able to claim title to your invention or work (see, in particular, the chapters on patents and copyright).

 For more information on loans, see the *Which? Essential Guide: Money Saving Handbook*. Information on small firm loans from the Department of Business Enterprise and Regulatory Reform is at www.berr.gov.uk/whatwedo/enterprise/enterprisesmes/info-business-owners/access-to-finance/sflg/page37607.html.

Case Study Jo

Jo's development and patent costs for her new cooler packs have spiralled and she needs more cash. She took out a £110,000 repayment mortgage on her house six years ago and has reduced the amount of the mortgage to £95,000 in that time. Her property is worth £220,000, so she applies to another bank for a new mortgage of £165,000, thus freeing up an extra £70,000 after her old mortgage is paid off.

Under the scheme, the Government guarantees to repay 75 per cent of the capital advanced by the lender plus six months interest, if the borrower defaults. The borrower pays a small fee as payment for the guarantee.

The SFLG scheme only applies to businesses with a turnover of less than £5.6 million and, at the time of writing, it has funding limits of up to £250,000. The vast majority of SFLG scheme loans are, however, between £5,000 and £100,000.

re-finance your existing mortgage, you may be able to release more cash. But you need to be careful not to over-extend yourself. The property market can be volatile and movements in property prices and interest rates could leave you exposed.

Government-assisted loans In an effort to encourage businesses, there are some state-sponsored schemes in place to help small businesses and start-ups. One example is the Small Firms Loan Guarantee (SFLG) scheme. This is aimed at encouraging financial institutions to lend to small businesses in cases where the borrower is unable to provide adequate security.

❝ A number of government bodies and other organisations award grants. Some only apply if the business is in a run-down area. ❞

OBTAINING FINANCE FROM GRANTS

There are a number of government bodies and other organisations that award grants to businesses or would-be entrepreneurs. The majority of grants are controlled by regional or municipal authorities and agencies. Indeed, in the case of some grant schemes, grant money is only available if the business in question is situated in a run down or deprived area.

 To find out more about the SFLG schemes, go to the Business Link website at www.businesslink.gov.uk/bdotg/action/detail?type=RESOURCES&itemId=1074447105.

For readers of this book, the most relevant category of grants would be those applicable to Small or Medium Sized Enterprises (SMEs). For example, in London, the London Development Agency (LDA) is the body responsible for promoting economic growth in London. It offers financing support for SMEs in a number of ways, including through vehicles such as the London Technology Fund and the Creative Capital Fund, the operation of each of which is outsourced by the LDA.

In the southeast of England, the South Eastern England Development Agency has a grant scheme for contributing finance to SMEs in its area, known as the Grant for Business Development.

In many cases, to be eligible for assistance it is necessary for the business itself to raise some funding and to use the grant to match or top-up that finance. The process of identifying relevant grant schemes that you might be eligible for can seem daunting as there isn't a national or harmonised grant system, but you can seek advice on which schemes are relevant by contacting your local Business Link office (see below).

FINANCING THROUGH EQUITY

If bank finance is difficult to come by or is insufficient for the needs of your business, and if you cannot fill the funding gap through grants, then you may have to explore other methods of financing.

Equity financing involves a third party investor paying money to you in return for shares in your company. The investor may also want, as part of the deal, to have representation in the management of the business, for example by having a permanent seat on the board of directors. So there is a price to pay for that investment.

Financing business through equity

There are a number of state-funded schemes aimed at helping businesses involved in innovation and product development, but they are continually evolving and therefore best researched when developing your idea. For established businesses that can hook up with someone from a university or other knowledge centre, government assistance is available through Knowledge Transfer Partnerships (KTPs) (see the box opposite, bottom).

The website for Business Link is www.businesslink.gov.uk. The equivalents to Business Link in the rest of the UK are Business Eye (Wales) at http://www.business-support-wales.gov.uk; Business Gateway (Scotland) at www.bgateway.com and Invest Northern Ireland (in Northern Ireland) at www.investni.com.

Case Study   Ron

Ron has set up a limited company and has filed patent and design applications in the name of that company. He owns all the shares in the company. He has approached his bank for a loan, but they are not prepared to grant him the extra funding he needs to develop the patented product without charging sky-high interest rates.

He decides he can live with giving away part of his company in return for the financial backing he needs, so Ron starts looking for an investor who will back him.

He posts blogs on various internet forums and business investment websites and makes contacts via investor groups on networking websites, including Facebook. Ron subsequently makes contact with three potential investors and after pitching to them he succeeds in securing a deal with an investor who is prepared to provide him with the money he needs in return for a 40 per cent stake in his company, so he agrees to transfer 40 per cent of the shares to them.

How much of your business should you give up?

Shares come with certain voting rights attached to them. So generally, the more shares you sell as a percentage of the shares in circulation, the more votes you are giving away. If you give up more than 25 per cent of your shares, you will be ceding what is termed 'negative control' to the investor. If you give up more than 50 per cent, you will have lost all but negative control yourself.

It is possible to enter into what is known as a 'shareholder's agreement' to govern the rights between shareholders in a company. Such agreements help clarify and govern dealings between the shareholders and can add contractual obligations that wouldn't otherwise apply without an agreement. For example, an

> **66 The more shares you sell as a percentage of the shares in circulation, the more votes you are giving way. 99**

For more information about KTPs visit www.ktponline.gov.uk. For more information about the help available in London see www.lda.gov.uk and for further details of the assistance providers referred to above see www.londontechnologyfund.com, www.ccfund.co.uk and www.investni.com.

agreement can be used to vary company law as it applies to voting rights between shareholders.

Naturally, if a business proves to be successful, the larger your stake in the company, the more dividend income you could receive from the shares or, if there is a sale, the more money you can realise from a sale of the company.

Therefore, there is a balance to be struck when financing your company through the sale of equity as there is a price to pay the more you give up in return for the finance. Viewers of the *Dragons' Den* television programme will know that this is very often the most contentious part of any negotiation (see box, opposite). The entrepreneurs pitching for finance will want to give up as little a share in their business as possible. The investors, however, will usually want to take the largest possible share of the business in return for the risk they are running with their investment and to make a meaningful return when they 'exit'.

Flexibility

Equity financing comes in many different forms. It is possible for companies to have different classes of shares, which, in turn, have different voting rights or privileges attached to them. These depend on the company's articles of association so you could make up your own. There could be, say, 'A shares', each of which counts as two shares for voting purposes, and 'B shares', which count as three votes on a particular type of resolution. Preference shares are a class of share that usually do not have voting rights but which have priority over other shares when it comes to dividend payments. Shareholder's agreements can also add flexibility by varying what company law would otherwise impose on the parties.

Disputes between company shareholders and directors are all too common. It is essential that you take independent legal advice from a solicitor (see pages 17-19 for finding a solicitor) before signing any agreement to give up equity or appoint third parties as directors of your company. You may otherwise be at risk in future of being ousted from your own company. A solicitor can also advise you about shareholders' agreements.

Negotiation

Most business transactions will be subject to some kind of negotiation about the terms of the deal. Negotiating the price of a shareholding is no different. Before the negotiation starts, it is sensible to set in your own mind the minimum you feel you must obtain from the negotiation. You also need to decide what level to pitch your opening bid to start the process. If an offer is made to you, then you may have to think on your feet and respond with a counter-offer. It is not sensible to generalise, because each negotiating scenario will be different. But a successful negotiation usually requires both parties to come away feeling that they have obtained something good and that is more likely if each party feels the other has compromised something. One-sided negotiations may leave the other party feeling aggrieved.

Business angels

Business angels are individuals who, whether on their own or as part of a syndicate with others, invest in businesses, including start-ups. In some cases they are content to be silent partners, but very often they will want to take an active role in helping with the business. As well as their own skills and experience, they may be able to exploit their existing contacts to help take the business forward. They may invest purely to make money or because they enjoy playing a part in helping to build a business.

Business angels will often have experience of the particular industry or sector that the business will be operating in. So when approaching business angels in the hope of raising finance from them, you should try to target mainly those who are likely to be attracted to your particular business sector.

Business angels will typically be prepared to invest down to relatively small sums of money. This differentiates them from venture capital investors, who are described overleaf.

The British Business Angels Association (BBAA) says that the main things business angels look for when investing are as follows:

- **The expertise and track record** of the founders and management.
- **The business's competitive edge** or unique selling point.
- **The characteristics and growth potential** of the market.
- **Compatibility between the management,** business proposal and

For more information about business angels, visit the BBAA website at www.bbaa.org.uk. The BBAA is the national trade association for business angel networks and is backed by the Department for Business, Enterprise and Regulatory Reform. See also www.envestors.co.uk, which matches investors to entrepreneurs.

Finance

the business angel's skills and investment preferences.

- **The financial commitment** of the entrepreneur.

Venture capital

Venture capitalists are people or organisations that invest cash in businesses in return for shares. They usually target companies that offer the prospect of high growth rates and where there is a good chance of achieving a public offering of shares or management buy out.

Venture capital investors are therefore generally more interested in investments with businesses that are already operating and have some kind of track

record. They are also likely to be interested only in larger investment sums (say £2 million or more), rather than the much smaller amounts that a typical start-up will be looking for.

❝ Venture capital investors are generally more interested in operational businesses that already have some kind of track record. ❞

The British Venture Capital Association (BVCA) website is at www.bvca.co.uk.

Pitching for finance

Whether you are seeing the bank manager about a loan, applying for a grant or trying to interest a group of investors in your business or idea, you have to be able to present yourself effectively – starting with your business plan.

DRAWING UP YOUR BUSINESS PLAN

When it comes to trying to persuade a bank or an investor to back your invention, your ideas or your business with hard cash, they will need to be convinced that lending you the money or making an investment will be a good thing for them.

The most effective way to do this is to prepare a business plan. After all, if you are serious about commercially exploiting your invention or idea you need to have a clear plan for how you can make it work.

A business plan is a document that explains what your business is about, who owns and runs it, what market your business is aimed at and who you will be competing with, what you intend to do with the business and what financial objectives and targets you have set.

Neither your bank manager nor your investor will be interested in the fact that you think your invention or business idea is the best thing since sliced bread. They see large numbers of business plans – many for similar things – so yours needs to be well structured to help it stand out.

A lender needs to know that it has a good chance of getting its money back and of profiting from making a loan by having you pay interest and/or fees. An investor will want to feel comfortable that there is a good chance of getting back not only their investment but of making a decent profit from it within a reasonable time frame. So don't get carried away by the technical excellence of your invention or idea. When it comes to raising finance, it is the money making potential that matters.

Business plans: structure

A typical business plan will tend to fall into three parts:

- **An executive summary.** This summarises the plan and should be no more than two pages long. It is analogous to the synopsis for a book and although it is usually placed at the beginning of the plan, it is best to write it last. Many investors or loan officers simply do not have time to wade through the detail of every business plan that comes across their desks. They may not even go beyond the executive summary. So it is crucial to get this part right.

- **The main section,** which describes in more detail what the business is, who owns or runs it, what market it operates in, who the competitors are, how the business will target its chosen market and what its numbers will look like. It must also demonstrate how the investor will be able to 'exit' and realise his or her investment.

- **An appendix.** To avoid disrupting the flow of the main part of the plan, it is advisable to group most of the figures and statistics into an appendix section at the end of the plan. This is where you set out the all-important numbers detailing financial information, such as your projected revenues, costs and profits.

The essential elements of a successful business plan

The executive summary
- A concise summary in one to two pages of the plan, which should outline your idea.

The main section
- Biographical details: an explanation of who you are (and if you are one of a number, who all of you are), your employment or business history, qualifications and how you came to be involved.
- Details of the product, idea or business proposition.
- The market and your potential competitors, giving the results of your market research.
- Why your product or proposition will be able to compete successfully, including any unique selling points (USPs) and details of where you are with IP rights protection.
- Your strategy for successfully exploiting the USPs and doing business.
- Your financial plans and financial projections including estimated revenues, costs and profits going forward for the next few years (putting the detailed figures relating to this in an appendix).
- The amount of money you need from the investor or lender and what that money is for.
- What is the exit strategy for equity investors: how and when will they be able to realise a return.

The appendix or appendices
- Containing detailed financial information.

For more information about business plans, see page 128. See also the *Which? Essential Guide* to *Working for Yourself.*

PREPARING TO PITCH

Now you are ready to start approaching potential lenders and/or investors, but a failure to pitch you and your business professionally can mean the difference between success or failure. It is not just your invention or business idea that will be the focus of attention, you will be scrutinised, too. No one is going to invest money in someone they cannot have confidence in.

Many of the things you will need to do are matters of common sense. Think of the process as a job interview. For example, you wouldn't usually show up to a job interview looking unkempt and scruffy, chewing gum and holding a cigarette. Upon meeting your interviewers you would try to greet them with a smile, look them in the eye and shake their hands firmly.

Meeting with or writing to a bank manager or a group of business angels is no different. You need to make a quick and favourable impression as you 'sell' yourself and your business idea. Just as you would hope to convince an employer that you are worth hiring over the other candidates, so you need to convince potential investors to lend you money or take a stake in your business. Successful pitching is a combination of:

- Your appearance.
- How you come across, what you say, how you say it, your timing.
- The way your written and visual materials are put together.
- Your commitment, and
- The content of your pitch.

You cannot predict in advance how your audience will react. Where you present to more than one person you may well find that there are differences in personalities and priorities among your audience.

It is true that some people are better at 'selling' themselves than others. But even if you are not a natural at it, there is no reason why you cannot put up a good performance and get your points across through lots of careful preparation.

Presenting your business plan: the pitch

The precise format for presenting your plan to investors or to a lender will depend on a number of factors. They may ask you to do it in a set format, such as a ten-minute PowerPoint presentation followed by a detailed question and answer session, or you may have a face-to-face interview about your business plan with no audio-visual presentation.

The important point is that you do not deviate too much from what they have asked for. So if they say they want a short presentation lasting no more than 15 minutes, do not prepare something that will take you 30 minutes. If they have stipulated no slides, don't give them slides.

A good idea or a good invention alone will not enable you to secure a loan or an investment. You must come across as credible so that an investor or lender will feel that you can be trusted with their money. See overleaf for advice on making a successful presentation.

Tips for a successful presentation

People have their own ideas about what makes for a good presentation. But read the following advice and you will not go far wrong.

Keep the overall structure clear and simple

- Start with a brief introduction. This is your chance to grab your audience's attention for the rest of what you have to say – or to lose it. Be creative. Try to think of an interesting way to start things off. Test your idea on a friend or colleague.
- Then give a description of what content you will be covering in your presentation. If you are using slides, a 'contents' slide will do that. Your audience needs to know what you intend to cover.
- Now move to the main content of your presentation. It can be helpful to break this down into, say, three parts so the audience has a sense of where they are and where the presentation is going. You need to get across:

  - The key points about your invention, product or idea and why you think it is commercially viable.
  - What you have done with it to date and what you are aiming to do going forward.
  - What you need your finance for.

  Your aim is to demonstrate that you have done your homework and understand that the invention or idea you have are a means to commercial success not an end in themselves.

- A brief summing up at the end draws it all together.
- At all costs, avoid a rambling, shapeless monologue!

Go for simplicity

- One of the most common mistakes people make with pitches is failing to realise the difference between the spoken word and the written word. If you write down a speech it may read very well from the page, but when you deliver it orally to an audience it can sound all wrong. Your potential investor can't see your words, so to be an effective communicator:

  - Use short sentences.
  - Avoid multiple syllable words.
  - Always think about how your words will sound to your audience.

  Once you have written your talk down, go through it and try to shorten every sentence.

- Compare the following two ways of saying pretty much the same thing. Read each of them out to someone and ask which one sounds better – it is not difficult to predict what they will say!

  'The market opportunities for exploitation of this product will necessarily increase, if as is our intention, the distribution network is expanded to embrace new territories.'

  'Our intention is to expand the distribution network. We will go into new territories with our product. As a result, we will be able to increase our market share.'

Using PowerPoint

- If you are going to use PowerPoint, make sure you use it properly. Design your slides with care and keep the slide content to a minimum.
- Do not use great long lists of bullet points and put them up on screen before you start talking about them. If you do, people won't hear what you say – they will be too busy reading the slide and feeling bored at the prospect of having to listen to you run through the points one after the other.
- Do not be over-elaborate with the animation of your slides, but do not be boring either. Illustrations, charts, tables and photos work well. Blocks of dense text do not.

Rehearsal and delivery

- The best way to ensure you do not 'freeze' up or get your timing wrong and the best way to ensure a confident presentation is to practise it over and over again – and out loud, too.
- Do not read your presentation from a script. Memorise it or use cues from PowerPoint or notes to help you deliver it.
- Time the presentation so that you know you can deliver it to the required time slot.
- If you have a camcorder, record yourself giving the presentation and critically review the footage – no matter how excruciating it may be to watch yourself in action. Use this process to eliminate irritating mannerisms in your delivery.
- Look at the audience as much as possible when you are delivering it and make plenty of eye contact with them.

Preparation, preparation, preparation

- Do your homework on what you say in your business plan.
- Know your numbers.
- Be able to talk about the market and your competitors.
- Be prepared for awkward questions.

You cannot anticipate everything that may be thrown at you, but like with a job interview, you can help yourself by looking prepared.

❝ Keep your presentation clear and simple, and prepare it thoroughly. ❞

GETTING HELP

There is plenty of advice available about writing business plans and what they should contain. If you know people who have successfully started up their own businesses or developed and marketed a new product or service, they are an obvious source of advice. The small business advisers who work for the main banks may not have themselves had much experience of setting up a business, but they will have worked with many businesses – successful and unsuccessful – and are likely to have useful advice to impart.

The internet also has a wealth of websites that can provide you with more information about the process of obtaining finance and how to prepare business plans. These websites will also direct you to places where you can seek face-to-face help – in many cases for free.

For help on starting and running a business generally, you will also find ready sources of advice and support, such as the network of Enterprise Agencies. These are locally based, not-for-profit organisations, which offer information, help and support to people on setting up and running new businesses. There is likely to be an Enterprise Agency in your area or the area you want to set up in (see below).

❝ If you know people who have successfully started up their own businesses, they would be a valuable source of help. ❞

The National Federation of Enterprise Agencies (NFEA) is the membership body for such agencies and has a list of members on its website at www.nfea.com. The National Federation of Small Businesses (NFSB), a trade association for small businesses, is at www.fsb.org.uk.

Launching your idea

If your business revolves around the development of a new product (as opposed to buying products from others), you will need to have it manufactured in order to take the business forward. If you are launching a service, you will need to set up everything so you can deliver the service. Alternatively, you can licence others to do so.

Manufacturing a product

In order to take forward an invention for a new product, you are likely to need models and prototypes. These are not only needed to test whether the product really works and to help with their manufacture, but it is much easier to pitch your business to potential investors and customers if you have something tangible to demonstrate to them.

CREATING PROTOTYPES

What exactly you produce in the early stages will depend on the nature of your invention or product. Of course, you may be able to produce a prototype or working model yourself, but if you have to go to a third party to do this for you, then you must be careful to protect the confidentiality of your invention.

The need for confidentiality in relation to patentable inventions and design protection is discussed on page 27. Remember to use a non-disclosure agreement (see the example on pages 28–31), with anyone who produces a prototype or model for you.

Another important factor is to ensure that there is no restriction on the use you can make of any model or prototype that has been produced for you. If you pay a third party to produce something for you, you need to ensure that they agree that all IP rights in the model or prototype are owned by you and not retained by them.

It is amazing how often this issue arises in practice and causes problems – even for well-known organisations. So always clarify who owns the IP rights before instructing the third party and not as an afterthought. The best place to do this is in a contract between you and the person who makes the model or prototype. Another good way of confirming the position is to send a letter or email asking them to confirm that they agree that all IP rights in the material belong to you and not to them.

COSTING

A product that costs too much to make relative to the price at which it can be sold is useless. So, of fundamental importance to the whole question of whether your idea or invention is viable, is whether you will be able to sell it at a

Strategies for pricing are examined in more detail later in this chapter on pages 135-7.

Case Study Andrew

Film maker George Lucas was the producer of the famous *Star Wars* science-fiction film and its subsequent follow-up movies. One of the iconic elements of the film was the distinctive white armour and helmets worn by Imperial stormtroopers.

Andrew had been responsible for producing the original armour and helmets for the film, first screened in 1977. In 2004, he started selling replicas of the armour and helmets over the internet. As a result, George Lucas's company Lucasfilm, which owns the rights to *Star Wars*, issued proceedings to stop him from doing so, alleging that he was infringing their copyright in the helmets and armour.

Among the issues that arose in the dispute was the question of ownership of the rights. It was unclear who owned the IP rights in the disputed works and what those rights were. A protracted, complicated and very costly legal battle followed in the US and UK, resulting in Andrew winning on many of the key points when the case went to trial in England. But the case did not stop there. What the Lucasfilm case demonstrates is how complicated the world of IP rights ownership can be if you don't clarify things from the outset.

price that generates a sufficient profit. But if you are launching a product, you cannot possibly assess pricing and profitability issues unless and until you know what it will cost to make the product ready for sale.

The first step is therefore to establish how much it will cost to manufacture your product. To obtain that information, you will have to do your research and consult with manufacturers and suppliers.

❝ The world of IP rights ownership can get very complicated if you don't clarify things from the very beginning. ❞

Costs associated with manufacturing

You need to be realistic about the costs of putting your product into production so as you work through this list be as objective as you can.

- **Further development costs, including additional prototypes or models.** It is quite likely that the product will continue to be developed and refined before it is ready to be manufactured. This will result from the need to overcome technical issues that arise or following feedback from potential customers or further market research.
- **Tooling/moulds for producing the products.** To make the product, it is likely that the factory producing it will

need to have either purpose-designed machinery or tooling created for the purpose. Alternatively, the existing plant can be modified or **retro-fitted** with the correct tooling or moulds. This will usually mean incurring up-front costs payable to the manufacturer before the product can go into production and before sales revenues can be generated.

- **Materials.** Raw materials will need to be sourced with which to make the products. The costs of these materials may fluctuate with commodity prices.
- **Labour costs.** Part of the unit cost of each manufactured item will be the labour costs associated with making it. Some products will be more labour intensive than others to produce.
- **Health and safety, hygiene and other manufacturing overheads.** If your product is a food or perishable item or something that is consumed by humans, you may be subject to all kinds of hygiene and other regulations – not only in relation to the conditions at the place of manufacture, but which also affect the subsequent handling and storage of the products. These can all push up costs.
- **Packaging.** This will have to be sourced, possibly independently from the manufacture of the product itself. It has to be designed and compliant with relevant trading laws and regulations.
- **Shipping, transport and logistical costs.** If the product is being manufactured overseas but sold in domestic markets or markets remote from the place of

Retro-fitted When an existing machine is fitted with new tooling or apparatus without having to install an entirely new machine

manufacture, the finished products will have to be shipped to where they are needed. They will also have to be transported from the place of manufacture to the relevant port or airport and again at the other end. They may have to be stored in a warehouse somewhere and insured against loss or damage.

- **Testing for compliance with relevant safety standards/CE marking.** Before many products can be sold legally in certain countries, they must meet certain basic requirements as set out in that countries' legislation. The legislation will usually stipulate the minimum requirements that must be met. Obviously, if the products cannot meet the relevant standard, they are not going to viable anyway. Also, it is not generally good enough that a pre-production prototype can meet the standard. The standards must be met by the finished product that will be on sale to the customer.

By the time the first production model rolls off the production line, a great deal of money will have been spent. So it is vital that you are confident from pre-production development and testing that the finished article will pass the relevant standards tests.

By their nature, some products will command a higher price because they are expensive to make. Other products may only be profitable if they can be sold in large volumes.

For the would-be entrepreneur, it is clearly a formidable undertaking to try to take an invention from concept, through development and to have it manufactured yourself. In many cases, you may be better trying to find a licensee who will do all this for you in return for royalty payments (see pages 166–72).

FINDING A MANUFACTURER

To help you find a manufacturer, there are sources of independent advice available, such as your regional Manufacturing Advice Service (MAS), which is a government-run service that supports British manufacturers. If you are looking to manufacture overseas, you might find the British Embassy in the territory concerned able to help. You can also use the internet (but see the warning box, above), where you will find an enormous amount of material to help you get started, including making direct contact with potential manufacturers and finding out where the relevant trade shows are.

 While numerous manufacturing companies, notably in Asia, can be found on the internet, you can't judge any of them from a website. Contact them, see what you get back and then, if you think they might be helpful, speak to someone at the company. Don't take anything at face value and always check a company's background (see below) before entering into business dealings.

❝ It may be worth finding a licensee to take an invention from concept to manufacture in return for royalty payments. ❞

Before employing a company, you will need to check the background of any potential manufacturer to try to ensure you are choosing the right one. This involves a variety of different types of research, such those listed overleaf.

 For more information about compliance with trading laws and CE marking, see pages 141-2.

- **Visit trade fairs** where traders in the field relevant to your goods or services are exhibiting and promoting their wares. You can pick up details of who manufactures particular products at these events and speak to people about their experiences. You may be able to obtain recommendations for certain manufacturers or, equally, you might learn which ones to avoid.
- **Order and examine samples of products** produced by the factories in question, which may tell you something about their quality control.
- **Read business reports** and make credit and other database searches, which may yield useful information about a manufacturer that could be good news or bad news.

In due course, you may need to travel to visit the manufacturer and see their factories for yourself.

❝ Visit trade fairs to find out who manufactures particular products. You may also find out who to use and who to avoid. ❞

To find your regional Manufacturing Advice Service (MAS) office, see www.mas.dti.gov.uk or, to find relevant trade shows, you could go to www.biztradeshows.com.

Pricing your product

A key element of any business is how to price your products and services correctly. Get this wrong and your business will be in trouble. You need to ensure you cover your costs and make something on top – but how do you decide what that margin should be?

PRICING AND MARKETING GO HAND IN HAND

The price that you can charge for a product or service in the market is essentially the sum of three things:

- **The costs you incur** in making and selling the finished product or in providing the service.
- **The level of reward** that you need to obtain in order to cover your costs and to generate a sufficient profit.
- **The value that your customers** place on the product or service you are providing for them.

Once you have worked out what your product or service is costing to make and deliver to the marketplace, you can use those figures and your business plan to assess the minimum price that you can charge for the product. You must ensure that this meets your costs and provides you with enough revenue on top.

This is relatively straightforward, but determining the value of your product or service to the customer is much harder to gauge accurately. In order to discover that 'value' figure, you must do your market research.

Cost pricing versus value pricing

It is commonly said that there are two types of pricing strategies: cost pricing and value pricing.

- Cost pricing is where you look at what something costs to make and you add a margin on top for what you need to make a profit. In other words, you set the price almost without regard to the customer. You are looking only at your costs and the return you need to cover those costs and give you a margin.
- Value pricing is where you look at the market and your position in it to try to assess what value customers will place on your product or service. This concentrates not so much on the costs of making the product or delivering the service, but rather how it is perceived in the market.

Research into prices and value is something that most of us do all the time. We do it when we visit a price comparison website, such as www.switchwithwhich.co.uk, to decide whether to change energy suppliers. We do it when we visit different retail stores to see who is selling the same pair of shoes at the cheapest price.

If your business offers a unique selling point over the competition or a special benefit that most of your rivals don't have, this will potentially justify charging a higher price. But your research might establish that while it may make your services more attractive to customers and make them more likely to buy from you, they may not be prepared to pay a higher price for it.

There is an obvious link between the pricing strategy you adopt for your product and the marketing strategy you pursue for selling and promoting it in the market. The types of marketing you use, your choice of media, the thrust of your advertising and how you position your product will need to be consistent with your pricing strategy.

Take care, too, that any research you undertake correctly targets the information you need. A flawed approach will inevitably lead you to a false reading, but, equally, it is very dangerous to ignore the importance of doing your research (see the case study, right).

To sum up, to determine the price you can charge for your product or service, do your market research so that you can understand the dynamics of the market,

Case Study John

John is considering buying a flat in a large city centre block, which comprises more than 400 flats. The block has been open for four years during which time there has been a change in the property market. He has been told by local estate agents what they think the market price is, but he wants to do some more research of his own.

He is shown around some flats on sale and notes their configuration and learns that the block consists of studios and one-bedroom flats. He visits one of the websites that shows the prices of all flats sold in the block over the past four years. Through this, he builds up a detailed picture of what the studios and one-bedroom flats have actually sold for over the years, including those he has visited. From this research he is able to form a view of the market value of the flats and so can enter into negotiations with the estate agent safe in the knowledge that he has a good understanding of the market. You can apply these principles to your business market research, too.

Information about market research and how you find out vital market information is covered on pages 146-62.

Case Study Charlie

Charlie believes that the local van hire services in his area are inflexible and that he can gain an edge by offering a drop-off and collection service, rather than requiring the customers to travel to his premises to collect and return their vehicles.

He studies the prices charged by his rival van hire businesses and the services they offer. None of them offer a drop-off and collection service. Charlie therefore decides that he will charge an extra £40 on each booking to cover the additional cost of the service and to make a small profit on it. He launches his service and makes much in his advertising of the free drop-off and collection service. But he achieves very few bookings. After a few weeks, he scraps the extra charge and the service and drops his prices to slightly below those of his main competitors. Bookings increase significantly.

Where did Charlie go wrong? He correctly believed that his drop-off and collection service was a benefit that made his business stand out from the competition. But he failed to carry out his market research beforehand. This would have established that while customers liked the service, they did not consider it important enough to justify paying an extra £40. Price was their most important priority. Charlie had overestimated the value of that service.

what your competitors are charging, what they are offering and how you can justify the price you are charging. Set the price too high, and your sales will suffer. Set it too low, and you will miss out on the profits you might otherwise have made.

❝Your research might show that customers won't pay a high price for your product or service, even if it is unique. ❞

Launching a service

Launching a service is likely to involve a different process compared to launching a new product. Much will depend, of course, on the nature and scope of the services you are offering. For example, a web-based business may require fewer staff than a business that requires numbers of telephone agents to generate sales.

Suppose you have an idea for a web-based dating agency using sophisticated software to match detailed criteria input by the people who sign up to it. That kind of service would require a great deal of work at the 'front end' to develop the software and website. A lot of resources would no doubt be needed to work with the software development team and web designers to perfect the operation of the website before going live with it. Yet once set up, it might require relatively little in the way of staff to operate the business. By contrast, a service for selling wireless broadband internet contracts might require a significant compliment of telephone operators and the management of a call centre.

HIRING SERVICES

If you are going to award a project to a software company to develop and provide you with bespoke software for your new business venture, then you need to apply similar principles to those you would apply in choosing a manufacturer or licensee. You would need to research and select some possible candidates to do the work, meet with them, preserve the confidentiality of your idea and look into their background. You may also need to negotiate with them to ensure that the IP rights to what they create and any improvements that you make to it belongs to your business and not to them.

If the new service you are launching involves employing or engaging people, you will need to decide whether you

“ When choosing a software company to work with, preserve the confidentiality of your idea during negotiations. ”

 Information on choosing a manufacturer is given on pages 133-4, and licensing is discussed on pages 166-72.

should be employing people full- or part-time, using temporary workers or possibly outsourcing these services to a third-party provider.

EMPLOYMENT LAW

It is beyond the scope of this book to go into any detail about employment law, but there are various websites you can consult for a basic introduction to the relevant issues you will need to cover. In the same way that learning more about how IP rights work will help you get the most out of the professionals you instruct, the same is true of employment matters.

For example, the Government's Advisory, Conciliation and Arbitration Service (ACAS) has a good website where you can download free booklets, such as 'Employing people – a handbook for small firms'. ACAS also runs a helpline and training sessions for employers at local level.

COSTS AND PRICING

The same principles apply to the costs and pricing associated with launching a service as they do to launching products (see pages 135–7), although the costs of providing services may be less. They may also involve less in the way of up-front costs than the development and manufacture of a new product.

If you are going to provide a service, you have to beware of trying to do so too cheaply if that adversely affects the quality of the service being delivered to your customers.

For example, if your service requires customers to make contact with you by telephone, don't skimp on the numbers of staff available to answer the phone. There is nothing more frustrating than being held in a 'queue' on the phone.

As soon as you look to engage or employ staff – on whatever basis – if possible, take legal advice on the implications of this. Employment laws in the UK are onerous and impose many burdens for businesses – in good times and in bad. There are ways of minimising the impact of those laws on your business, but you are likely to get into difficulties if you are not careful. Becoming an employer involves taking on all kinds of responsibilities, including health and safety, tax, National Insurance and employment protection rights.

More official guidance of all aspects of employment rights can be sought via www.direct.gov.uk/en/Employment/index.htm. The ACAS website is www.acas.org.uk.

If you are launching a service over the internet and have had a web development company set up the site for you, make sure that you have performance tested the site properly before launching it and done your best to iron out bugs and problems. In the internet age, people are fickle and have very limited tolerance for poorly performing websites. If a site is user unfriendly, unresponsive or full of bugs, you may lose customers and they are unlikely to come back.

" In the age of the internet, people are fickle and have very limited tolerance for poorly performing websites. "

Legal matters

When you launch a new business, you will need to navigate a legal minefield. This may include making sure that your products are safe and comply with the relevant trading laws. This section deals with this as well as flagging up some other legal matters you need to be aware of.

COMPLIANCE WITH TRADING LAWS

We live in a world where the number and complexity of rules and regulations governing virtually every area of activity continues to grow. The EU, in particular, sends out numerous directives and rules and trading standards departments and government enforcement bodies can, in some cases, be zealous in imposing these rules. So you cannot afford to ignore them.

Whatever type of product you are proposing to produce and sell, you can be sure there will be some kind of legislation that you will need to comply with. For example, food products are subject to the relevant food labelling legislation. The packaging of such products must provide certain information by law or it will be illegal to sell it.

Failure to comply with trading laws can lead to prosecutions and possible fines or, in extreme cases, even imprisonment. But even where the end result is not so drastic, breaching trading laws can have an adverse PR effect on your business. It can put off investors and customers and attract unfavourable news coverage. This is compounded by the internet where a bad news story can remain at large coming up on Google searches for months, even years after the event.

So take trading laws and compliance with standards seriously.

> ❝ Whatever the product, there is sure to be legislation affecting it. ❞

Case Study | Jane

Jane has invented a patented folding mechanism for a pushchair. She has found a licensor to take on the manufacturing and promotion of the pushchair.

Before it can market the pushchair in the UK, the licensor must ensure that it complies with the relevant legislation. Pushchairs are subject to the Wheeled Child Conveyances (Safety) Regulations 1997, which requires them to comply with British Standard 7409:1996. This means that they must be tested in accordance with the requirements of that Standard and satisfactorily meet the test criteria. They must also comply with the Furniture and Furnishings (Fire)(Safety) Regulations 1988 and be sufficiently fire resistant.

Jane's licensor must ensure that the product complies with these requirements before supplying them to retailers.

CE marking

Within the EU, there is also a system known as 'CE marking'. If you look at many everyday items closely you will see that they have the CE mark on them. This denotes that they meet the relevant safety and/or product standards designated by a particular EU Directive. There are around 25 such Directives in force covering an infinite variety of products, ranging from computers and radio equipment to lifts and specialised medical devices.

If you are going to oversee the manufacture of your own products, you need to be aware of the relevant legislation applicable to your products.

Help and guidance

There are a number of organisations that specialise in testing products for compliance with relevant safety and other trading laws and standards. Examples are the British Standards Institution (BSI), SGS and TUV (see below). The BSI is a long-established organisation that develops industry standards for products and services and certifies them. It is also involved in product testing and training. Together with the SGS and TUV, these organisations have divisions that are experienced in particular sectors and have a lot of specialised knowledge. It may pay dividends to seek advice or input from such organisations while you are developing your products. This will help ensure that potential standards problems are spotted as early as possible in the development process.

In some cases, there might even be a fundamental flaw in the design of your product that will make it almost impossible to pass the relevant safety standard. If that were to be the case, better to find out as early as possible before spending a fortune on patent protection and development.

DATA PROTECTION LAWS

If you are providing a service to members of the public or selling goods directly to them, it is likely that you will capture personal information about them, such as their names, addresses and contact details, and also possibly some biographical information, such as their date of birth and marital status.

If you run a business that captures such information, you will need to be aware of your responsibilities under the Data Protection Act 1998 (DPA). This imposes a number of legal obligations on businesses that hold or process such personal data.

Unless your business is 'exempt' under the DPA (which will be rare for most businesses), you will have to register with the Information Commissioner's Office

 Further information about CE marking can be found at the website of the Department of Business Enterprise and Regulatory Reform at www.berr.gov.uk. See also the BSI website at www.bsi-global.com.

(ICO). This involves sending in a completed notification form and a small fee (currently £35) to the ICO. Notifications can be made online or you can request a form. Even if you are exempt from registration, you will need to make sure that you process any personal data in accordance with the DPA. For example, you should not disclose people's personal data to third parties without their consent and you must exercise care with how you store and use personal data.

For information on the obligations and requirements of the DPA, visit the ICO's well-structured website (see below), where there is plenty of useful guidance. You can also download various guides on selected topics, such as handling data stored from CCTV images, how to deal with requests from the public for information and a host of other subjects.

LAWS AFFECTING INTERNET BUSINESSES

The EU has been quick to get its legislative tentacles into the new world of electronic commerce. A flood of new laws has come out of Europe, which businesses who use the internet need to be aware of. They include three laws designed to 'help' govern the world of e-commerce.

- The Consumer Protection (Distance Selling) Regulations 2000 (as amended).
- The Electronic Commerce (EC Directive) Regulations 2002.
- The Privacy and Electronic communication Regulations (EC Directive 2003).

 It is important that businesses comply with these various regulations. You should seek legal advice from a solicitor about your position (see pages 17–19 for finding suitable legal support). Employ a solicitor to run a website 'health check' to ensure you are complying with the law. Ask for an estimate as to how much this will cost you. It need not cost a great deal of money, but it could prevent you from being investigated by trading standards or running into other difficulties as a result of breaching the law.

 The websites for BSI, SGS and TUV are: www.bsi-global.com, www.uk.sgs.com and www.tuvps.co.uk. The ICO website is www.Ico.gov.uk.

These regulations impose various legal requirements on businesses that are selling to consumers via the internet and other 'distance selling' means. The Office of Fair Trading (OFT) has produced a guide called 'A short guide to business on distance selling', which helps to explain what this legislation is about and what requirements it imposes on businesses.

TERMS AND CONDITIONS OF BUSINESS

Before you can sell anything to anyone – be it products or services – you must have suitable terms and conditions in place governing the terms of the contract you will be entering into.

When you buy from your supplier, you will usually have to sign up to their terms of business. When you sell to your customers, you want ideally to ensure that they buy from you on your terms. This means that you have the opportunity to impose the most advantageous possible contractual terms.

Of course, there are inevitably rules and regulations governing what can and cannot go into contracts and the restrictions are more onerous in relation to businesses that deal with consumers rather than other businesses. However, the important point is that a badly drafted set of terms and conditions can leave you in a very unsatisfactory

position. It could mean that your position in a legal dispute is ambiguous and it is difficult to recover money from an errant customer. Or worse, you might find that your contract is unenforceable because it breaches consumer protection legislation. For further information on the subject, go to the OFT website (see below).

It is a sound investment to have a suitable firm of solicitors draft a set of terms and conditions for you. In most cases, they will already have a suitable precedent, which may need tweaking for your particular circumstances. Again, you should be able to obtain a fixed quote in advance and this should not be a costly exercise. A proper, legally compliant set of terms and conditions will almost certainly more than pay for themselves very quickly, especially if you ever have a contractual dispute where you need to rely on them.

❝A badly drafted set of terms and conditions can leave you in a very unsatisfactory position and you could end up losing money.❞

The OFT's website is at www.oft.gov.uk and to find more information for consumer protection legislation, simply key in those words in the search panel.

Know your market

It is pointless to pursue an idea if there is no market for your product or service. Similarly, no one is going to invest in a business unless they believe there is a market for what that business will be supplying. Identifying the market is an essential element in business planning. Having identified that there is a market, you need to decide how you can effectively target that market.

Is there a market?

You may have invented something that you think is innovative and you are so convinced that it will be successful that you have already filed a patent application to protect it. But have you investigated whether there really is a commercial market for the product?

If you have not, it may turn out that you have wasted your money. However, once you have filed your application, you have at least protected your invention as best you can from having it copied by someone else. You need to focus on the commercial aspects of your invention. Will it sell? Can you, or someone that you appoint make it profitable?

Similarly, where you plan to start up a business that involves providing services, exactly the same principles apply. Your service must appeal to a sufficient market of potential customers and it must be capable of being operated profitably.

To determine whether or not there is a market out there and what it is, you need to do some research.

> ❝Market research can take many forms, including talking to or getting data on existing customers, or interviewing potential consumers.❞

MARKET RESEARCH

As its title suggests, market research is the process of investigating relevant aspects of the market for goods and services. The aim of such research is to provide the researcher with knowledge of customer needs, desires and issues so that products, services and advertising can be more effectively targeted. Your research may even demonstrate that there is no market for a particular product or service, or that there is too much competition.

Market research can take many forms. It does not just consist of one of those irritating people with a clipboard who tries to stop you in the street when you are running late for an appointment.

For example, when you finish a package holiday, you will often be asked to complete a feedback form. That form is ostensibly asking you about your experiences on the holiday you have just finished. But it will usually seek additional information from you for market research purposes, such as how many holidays you take each year, what the average duration of those holidays is, and what type of holiday you like. The holiday company is trying to build a profile of its customers to help fine tune its marketing and targeting of holidays.

Other methods of gathering market research data include:

- Asking existing customers to complete survey forms online or in paper form in return for being entered in a prize draw.
- Sending researchers with those clipboards out on the streets to interview consumers face to face.
- Conducting 'focus group' meetings with consumers under the supervision of a facilitator.
- Telephoning people at home or at work to ask them questions.
- Operating customer loyalty cards, such as Tesco Clubcard and Nectar, which are instruments for gathering an enormous amount of data on customer shopping habits.

GATHERING MARKET RESEARCH INFORMATION

If you have not yet started trading and are still developing your product or business idea, then there are three ways you can gather market research information:

- Engaging the services of a professional researcher or agency to advise you, to conduct research for you and to present and interpret the results.
- Trawling the internet and other sources, such as a business library, to see if there is any published research data that you can make use of – whether for free or by buying it.

- Conducting your own market research.

You can, of course, employ a combination of these methods.

> **“Use a professional market researcher, find published data or undertake your own.”**

Using professional market researchers

Market research companies not only conduct research according to established principles and statistical criteria, but they can also advise on the appropriate strategies you could take for gathering the right information.

The advantage of seeking such professional help is that the results ought to be more robust and accurate than if a do-it-yourself approach is adopted. Another advantage is that a favourable report from a recognised market research company may well help convince a bank or investor to support your business proposition. The fact that you have taken market research so seriously will help show them that you are taking a commercial approach. Also, a report from a recognised market research company is likely to carry more weight than home produced research.

The downside, of course, is that turning to the professionals will cost

Briefing a market research agency

The first thing you need to do is find some possible agencies or professionals to approach. The Market Research Society (MRS) and the Research Buyer's Guide (RBG) are good starting points for identifying suitable candidates.

Once you have identified two or three agencies that you want to work with, have a meeting with each one to brief the agency about your product or service so they can understand and advise on what exactly is needed. This initial meeting should, if possible, be free of charge and without obligation. You may also need to ask the agency to sign a non-disclosure agreement (see pages 28-31) if there is a risk of your passing them information of a confidential nature.

After the meeting, each agency should produce a costed proposal, possibly to be implemented in a number of stages. At that point you have to decide whether to go with any of them or not.

---

money and the larger the scope of the research, the more expensive it will be. In the start-up phase of a business or at the project development stage where cash is tight, it simply may not be practical to incur such costs.

Using existing market research data

By trawling the internet or visiting a business library it may be possible to dig out statistical and other research data that could support what you are doing. For example, the Office for National Statistics (ONS) has a wealth of information available free online (see below). You can even drill down into detailed statistics for individual post code areas and boroughs from their website.

In addition to free information available in libraries and over the internet, you can also pay for reports or market research data published by private bodies. These include organisations such as Global TGI, an international network of market and media research surveys (see below).

The obvious danger of relying too heavily on information viewed or bought 'off the shelf' is that it may not be wholly relevant to the particular product or service you are proposing to start offering. But it is likely to be cheaper than commissioning your own professional research from scratch.

 For more information about market research see the Market Research Society website at www.mrs.org.uk and the Research Buyer's Guide at www.rbg.org.uk. The website of the ONS is www.statistics.gov.uk and that for Global TGI is www.tgisurveys.com. See also the MRS website: www.mrs.org.uk.

Carrying out your own market research

Although it is unlikely that you will be able to achieve the kind of national coverage, sophistication or statistical purity of a professional agency, if money will not allow you to use one, there is no reason why you cannot go out and conduct some useful market research of your own. Indeed, in practice this will often be the only option for the budding inventor or would-be entrepreneur.

At its most basic, you can conduct research on your family, friends and work colleagues. But you will almost certainly need to get out there and work harder than that. There is nothing to stop you taking your clipboard out on the streets and trying to do your own basic fieldwork, but if you do, you need to think carefully about what it is you want to achieve from the research.

If you are going to ask people questions by means of a survey, then you need to make sure that you ask them the right questions. Some of the pitfalls and points to think about can be illustrated by the case study, overleaf.

Making your own market research count

If you are going to do your own market research and design a survey, you need to think very carefully about what it is you want to achieve. Otherwise, the whole exercise may be a waste of time or – worse – give you a false result and raise false hopes that there is a market for what you are doing.

In the case study, overleaf, Teri would have been better off taking her survey to different localities and perhaps using survey points in an affluent area, a less expensive area and a poorer area. This might have enabled her to discover, for example, whether she should target salons only in the more affluent areas or whether her invention would appeal more widely.

Teri's case study relates to a purely fictitious potential product for the hair salon market. But the principles are equally applicable to market research for any type of product or service.

The key point with market research surveys of this type is to think carefully about the information you want to find out from your research and to design questions that will hopefully elicit the right information – but without distorting the results or 'leading' the respondents to their answers.

RESEARCHING COMPETITORS

Another aspect of any business plan you prepare will be the part showing that you know who your competitors are and what they are doing. It is very rare that you will be entering into any kind of market where there is no competition present or no potential competitors. This is so even if you have an innovative new product. When James Dyson introduced his bagless vacuum cleaner, there may have been no other bagless cleaners on the market, but there were plenty of traditional cleaners to compete with.
(Continued on page 154)

149

Case Study Teri

Teri has noticed how uncomfortable it is when she has her hair washed at her hairdresser. She has to lie back in a chair and balance her neck on the solid, sculpted edge of the washbasin for the duration of the process. Furthermore, she has read stories in the newspaper about people being injured and bruising their neck when lying back in this awkward position at the hairdresser. Teri realises that the 'lie back' method appears to be the standard for most hair salons she has visited, which sets her thinking about what could be done about it.

She has the idea to design a retractable, hygienic fitting to interface with the basin, which eases the strain on a person's neck and which makes the whole experience more comfortable. The fitting can be left in place between washes and uses a disposable but recyclable cover.

Her belief is that in the initial stages of the product's sales life, if a salon has this fitted, it will be a selling point to potential customers. But she reasons that as more and more salons take up the product, it will become a standard piece of kit, and become an essential item – thus guaranteeing repeat sales. The bespoke disposable covers will be an ongoing market, too, and provide a constant income stream for Teri's business.

Teri's research

Having identified her overall target market, before she can prepare a business plan or spend money on investigating patent and design protection, Teri needs to do some basic market research, without revealing too much about the detail of her invention. She needs to know whether or not her idea will really be attractive to potential customers within her target market of the professional hair salon and how big that interested market is likely to be.

Finding out the size of the potential market is something Teri can do using the internet. She finds websites where the results of research are published and checks out statistical data gathered by various bodies. This establishes that there are around 6,000 hairdressing salons in the UK, each with an average of 3.5 basins. So she knows that potentially there are over 20,000 basins in hair salons in the UK that could potentially be fitted with her product.

However, this tells her nothing about whether there is likely to be any demand for her product among those salons. To find this out, she decides to do her own research by means of a survey.

Teri chooses three hair salons in her high street and starts asking people who come out of them the following questions:

- When you have your hair washed in a hair salon, do you find it uncomfortable to have to lean your neck back against the basin?
- If the answer to Q1 is 'yes', do you think it would be a good idea if someone invented a product that could remove this discomfort?

Teri is excited by the responses she gets. Almost all of those questioned who co-operate with her, reply 'yes' to both questions. She thinks this indicates that there is a market for her product. In fact, it shows no such thing.

What did Teri get wrong?

The first problem with what Teri has done is that her chosen survey respondents may not be a true reflection of the market. The profile of customer coming out of a salon in a particular street might well be very different to the profile of customers in another area of town. The salons she chose might be marketed at premium-priced customers or they might be the opposite. Take care to survey the right cross-section of potential customers.

The second problem with Teri's research is that her survey questions were not very well constructed and were almost bound to produce the results they did. She has not identified whether the hair wash experience is really that important to the average customer. Nor has she established how important it is compared to other factors, such as price and service.

This is because she introduced the problem of the hair washing experience into her first question – it was a 'loaded' question. As a result, she artificially placed the problem at the forefront of the respondent's mind when, in reality, it might rank very low on a typical customers' list of priorities.

Nor has she elicited any information that test whether customers would be prepared to pay more for a hairdressing experience that involved a more comfortable hair wash.

Finally, she hasn't taken the opportunity to gather any additional information that could be of use to her later on. For better constructed questions that Teri should have asked, see her continued case study, overleaf.

By chance, Teri subsequently met a marketing professional at her tennis club and without giving away details of her idea, was able to obtain some tips. She has realised that her first survey was not particularly well designed. Armed with his advice, she has designed a new survey and created a new set of questions.

1 Do you have your hair cut at a hair salon?
(This question ensures that the person being questioned is actually relevant in the first place. If they do not have their hair cut at a salon, there is no point in questioning them further. They don't form part of the relevant target market.)

2 Do you always go to a particular salon?
(This question identifies whether they are regulars or whether they have no affinity to any particular salon. It will enable Teri to know roughly what percentage of hair salon customers are regulars or ad hoc attendees.)

3 Can you list the four most important reasons why you keep going back to that salon? [or, if respondent is not a regular: the four reasons you choose any particular salon?]
(This question is aimed at identifying the most important positive factors that attract customers to a particular hair salon.)

4 Can you list the four things that you most dislike about going to the hairdresser?
(This is the key question that Teri needs answering. It will identify – unprompted – whether customers attach any real importance to their hair washing experience. If they do not mention 'uncomfortable hair washes' as being one of the factors in answer to this question, it strongly suggests that this isn't a significant factor. If it isn't a significant factor, then the chances are, Teri has invented a product for which there is no real need or demand.)

[If discomfort when having hair washed is one of the items on the respondent's list in answer to question 4, proceed to ask questions 5 and 6.]

5 If another salon had a basin that made your hair wash a more comfortable experience, would you be more likely to book with that salon than your usual salon or would it make no difference?
(For those who have identified their hair washing discomfort as a factor, this question will elicit just how important a factor this is and whether or not it is sufficiently important to prompt the customer to change salons to one that was using Teri's product.)

6 Would you be prepared to pay more to have a more comfortable hair wash experience at your salon?
(This question is aimed at probing whether the hair wash discomfort factor is such that customers would be willing to pay extra to deal with it.)

The results of Teri's survey were disappointing. After the excitement of her first survey, she now realised that while people liked the idea of making their visit to the hairdresser more comfortable, when it came to stumping up more cash, they didn't see the hair wash as sufficient justification. Teri felt relieved that she had found this out before investing more time and money in the idea, but she had nevertheless learned from the process and was spurred on by it to think up something new.

❝ Your market research might help by revealing a flaw in the product or service that spurs you on to thinking again and coming up with something new. **❞**

How your competitors react to your entry into the market with a new product or service will be an important factor in your ability to be successful. Will they cut prices and aggressively promote their goods or services in order to damage your venture? Will they be able to copy what you are doing and do it cheaper or better themselves?

If you are going to make a success of your product or service, you have to be able to deal with the competition. You can't do that if you don't know who they are. If you are pitching for financial backing, you will not impress a banker or business angel if you do not know about your competitors.

There are many ways to research the market for your competitors:

- Local business directories.
- Google searches.
- Trade mark searches.
- Walking the high street.
- Visiting competitors.
- Phoning competitors.
- Looking at your competitors' websites.
- Obtaining quotes where appropriate to see what the competition is offering.

You need to use your imagination and to do your homework to try to find out the competition's strengths, weaknesses, what they charge, what their product does or how their service works and which area they operate in. You can then assess what your unique selling points (USPs) are when you start competing with them. In order to succeed in a competitive marketplace, you have to offer a reason why customers should buy from you rather than the competition.

❝ You need to know who your competitors are and how they might react. ❞

AN ONGOING PROCESS

Market research does not finish with the launch of a new business, product or service. It is something that should continue regularly. Broadly speaking, there are two types of ongoing research:

- **Quantitative research,** which is designed to find out how many customers (and what sort of customers) are buying or have bought particular goods or services. It often involves data collection and statistical analysis.
- **Qualitative research,** which aims to discover either why people buy or like particular goods or services, or why they don't buy them.

To find out more about market research, go to www.qualitativeresearch.uga.edu/QualPage/, which has a page of web links to other sites dealing with the subject.

Targeting your market

Once you have established that there is a market for your products or service and you know what that market is and what competition you have, you can plan how you would actually market and sell your products or services. If you have appointed a distributor or licensee, you may not have to worry so much about this.

MARKETING

Depending upon the type of business you are engaged in, there a number of different ways you can promote your products or services. However, before doing this you need to consider:

- **Whether you will be doing everything yourself** or appointing licensees, distributors, agents or franchisees, or a combination of these (see pages 166–80).
- **What protection you have in place** for your IP rights (see Chapters 2–5).

As you market your products or services you need to make sure that this is consistent with your IP rights; for example, ensure you use the logo in the form in which you have registered it as a design or a trade mark. If you change something that could affect your IP protection, such as renaming a product or your business or moving to a different logo, you may need to file a fresh trade mark registration.

If you have appointed distributors, licensees or other third parties who will be responsible for marketing your products or services, you will need to protect the integrity of your brand and other IP rights. In your contract with these parties you should retain a semblance of control over how they use your IP rights. You will also need a manual setting out your policy for usage of trade marks in advertisements and marketing materials (see page 179).

Marketing materials

Some basic essential marketing elements you will need to have are:

- Website and email contact addresses, contact telephone numbers and office addresses.
- Point of sale materials, brochures, price lists.
- Samples of the product; for example, if you are in the business of making books, it would mean bound proof copies.
- A well-designed website.
- Business stationery bearing your business or brand name, including notepaper, invoices, delivery notes, business cards, signage.

Direct marketing

Direct marketing is a term used to describe a type of marketing that directly targets the potential customer rather than doing so through other means, such as advertising where an advert is placed aimed at a target audience. This can be achieved by posting hard copy materials direct to potential customers (so-called 'junk mail'), or its online equivalent – direct email marketing.

Direct mail or email have something of a bad reputation and may seem wasteful. Indeed, the vast majority of unsolicited mail is binned immediately and in the case of emails will be deleted before they are even read – assuming they are not filtered out as 'spam' before they even arrive.

However, the very fact that everyone's post and inboxes continue to be invaded by large quantities of unsolicited mail and emails, suggests that these techniques do achieve results. To some organisations, even a very small 'conversion' rate among recipients into those who buy rather than bin, can make a direct marketing campaign worthwhile. Moreover, these days, specialist email marketing companies have evolved all sorts of sophisticated techniques for getting around spam filters and ensuring that a high percentage of their clients' emails reach their intended targets.

Nevertheless, using unsolicited mass emails like this can rebound on a company's reputation. By contrast, permission marketing, where you ask the customer if they want more information about your products or services by requesting them to opt in to receive that information, may achieve better results with less risk. With permission marketing, you are at least targeting people who have indicated they might be receptive to your emails and have filtered out those who clearly wouldn't be.

> ❗ The Data Protection Act 1998 imposes various rules about the use that may be made of personal data (names, email addresses, telephone numbers and postal addresses). Regulatory bodies, such as the Office of Communications (Ofcom), enforce the regulatory regime for telephone marketing. Before using mailing lists or doing any direct marketing you need to make sure you are not breaching any of these laws or rules. If you hold personal data in the course of business you may also need to register with the Information Commissioner as a data controller. Seek legal advice from a solicitor about such matters.

Telemarketing

Similar to direct mail, this involves telephone calls to potential customers.

 Further information about data protection can be found at the Information Commissioner's website at www.ico.gov.uk and at Ofcom's website at www.ofcom.org.uk.

Again it can take the form of merely calling a list of numbers or it could be second stage telemarketing (also known as segmentation) using leads generated from a prior blanket calling exercise.

Sales visits

This is self-explanatory – it involves making visits to potential customers. These could be the result of cold calling or writing to the potential customer beforehand to try to arrange a meeting. If someone is prepared to meet you, there is a better chance that he or she might be more receptive to your message than if you turn up on spec. The approach you adopt depends on the type of customer and the type of product or service you have.

Sales promotions

You could offer a local retailer some stock at a discounted price along with some promotional materials, or you could have a stall or demonstrator set up to promote the product to customers at particular retail outlets. Such promotions are a good way of bringing your product to the attention of the public. As well as gaining exposure for the product, it might act as a crude form of market research since you would be able to gauge first hand how the product is viewed. If it is successful, it might help you win orders from the place where the demonstration is being run.

Sponsorship

Sponsorship, such as for sports grounds, sports people, films, celebrities, awards ceremonies and charity functions, can raise awareness of a brand and be used to help promote it. Sponsorship is not just for multi-national companies or televised sports events. It can also be done cheaply at a local level. But it must have a strategy behind it – if you sold waterproof hiking jackets, you wouldn't sponsor a sunless tanning salon.

Trade shows and exhibitions

Depending on whether your target market is businesses or consumers (or both) there are various trade shows for particular types of products or services where you can pay to take a stand. While you are likely to be alongside your closest competitors at such an event, the benefit of being there is that the visitors milling around are likely to be there because they are interested in the type of products and services that are on display. Trade magazines are good sources for learning about forthcoming exhibitions and trade shows (see also the box below).

> ❝ Sales promotions bring your product to public attention and show how it will be viewed. ❞

To find details of exhibitions and trade shows, there are plenty of websites such as www.exhibitions.co.uk. Your local Business Link office will also have information about exhibitions and shows: see www.businesslink.gov.uk.

Referrals

Obviously one of the most important ways of promoting anything is for it to be recommended by those who have bought or used it. The prerequisite for this is that you must supply a good product or a great service. You can leave it to the satisfied customer to spread the word (people love recommending things to their friends or colleagues), or you can go further and contact the customer asking if you can use a testimonial from them.

Referral networks

Where your business is complementary rather than in competition to another type of business, you may be able to form referral networks whereby they refer customers to you and vice versa. For example, a builder may recommend a particular tile shop and the tile shop may reciprocate by recommending a particular builder. Or a website supplying business training videos may carry an advert for a favoured recruitment agency and the recruitment agent may recommend the training company to its own candidates and clients.

Achieving awards

Some businesses specifically target achieving awards so they can advertise the fact they have done so and promote a positive image to the outside world.

Affiliate marketing

There are several internet companies nowadays that have affiliate marketing businesses. These enable you to appoint 'affiliates', which could be anyone from another company to individuals operating their own websites. The affiliate places click-through adverts for your website on their own websites. When customers reach your site via these affiliate sites, their actions can be tracked and commission paid to the affiliate for any sales generated. Becoming an affiliate could be a useful means of generating extra income for your business from your website and is remarkably easy to set up (see box, below).

PUBLIC RELATIONS (PR)

PR is about managing the reputation of an organisation (or individual) and attempting to protect and promote that reputation. It can be used proactively to boost the client's image and reputation and to present the client in a favourable light. If an event occurs that threatens to damage a client's reputation or image, then PR has a reactive role to play in trying to counter any negative stories that may arise.

If money allows, you may wish to seek professional PR help, but it is equally possible to do your own public relations work.

 An example of an affiliate marketing business is TradeDoubler whose website at www.tradedoubler.com explains more about how the business works. See also www.iabuk.net, the website of the trade association for internet advertisers (the Internet Advertising Bureau), which has some helpful resources and information.

- **Cultivate relationships with the press or media** in the hope that when the time comes you will receive favourable or sympathetic coverage or to facilitate the placing of favourable stories about you and your idea.
- **Write press releases.** These are self-serving documents written with the aim of informing the press or media of a story in the hope that they will publish it or take extracts from it.

PR is very much an ongoing art rather than being about one-offs. So it may be best – if you can afford it – to pay a PR agent a retainer on a monthly or quarterly basis to advise you. This means that they ought to be incentivised to look out for your interests on an ongoing basis. To find out more about what PR agents can do for you, arrange to visit a few to discuss your requirements on a no obligation basis.

Working with creative agencies

To build a fruitful relationship with creative agencies, such as **PR** and marketing professionals or advertising agencies, bear the following in mind:

- Make sure that whoever you work with really grasps what your business is about and understands the relevant market that you are competing in. If they don't really understand what you do and don't know the market, they can't possibly help you reach or influence your target audience.
- You would expect them to do some research, but try to help them with a proper and thorough brief.
- Try to meet with them on a regular basis and make sure you update them on developments, changes and other information that you think they ought to know.
- If you are trying to gain press coverage, you need to be responsive when your **PR** agent contacts you with a possibility of getting a story about your business into the media – newspapers, radio and television are fast-moving mediums and there are always a number of stories competing for attention. If you want to get coverage, you need to move quickly and give the matter your attention or the opportunity may quickly be lost.
- You are paying a **PR** agent in part for the privilege of exploiting their media contacts. But there is no reason why you shouldn't cultivate your own journalistic or other contacts in the search for favourable publicity.

For more information about PR, go to the Chartered Institute of Public Relations (CIPR), the main industry body for the PR industry, website at www.cipr.co.uk.

ADVERTISING

Advertising is generally a means of informing potential customers that your product or service is available and of trying to persuade them to buy from you. Advertising can be carried out in many different forms: in newspapers, magazines, billboards, on vehicles, on sandwich boards worn by people, and on promotional items such as pens, on TV, radio, the internet. The list is varied.

Wherever possible, make advertising part of a planned and targeted campaign, otherwise there is a risk that the money spent on doing it will be wasted and the advertising ineffective.

When you see an advert appear on television, it may be over in a few seconds. The message it conveys may be very simple. However, what you do not see is the considerable research and planning that has almost certainly gone into devising the campaign before the advert was even created.

If you are about to launch a new product or service on the market as a start-up or relatively new business, it is unlikely you will have the funds for a sophisticated television, cinema and radio campaign. But even with a limited budget and a modest amount of advertising to do, the principles are exactly the same (see the box, opposite).

Internet presence

An internet presence is often critical these days. Search engine 'sponsored links' – otherwise known as 'adwords' – are a form of advertising that can be found on search engines such as Yahoo! and Google. You can 'bid' for the rights to sponsor particular search terms that are used by consumers when making Google or similar searches. Either do this directly by setting up an account with the relevant search engine and reading how the process works on their website, or your advertising agency, should you be employing one, can do this for you. Where those terms are keyed into the search box, a sponsored link appears alongside the normal search results. This is a way of having your goods or services advertised prominently on the internet.

Jargon buster

The AIDA principle An acronym for:
- Attention: the headline or introduction grabs the attention of the target audience
- Interest: having grabbed attention, the advert maintains interest
- Desire: The advert explains how your product service benefits the customer, such as being cheaper, better, easier to use, more fun
- Action: invite customers to buy the product or service immediately or to contact you via the number or address given in the advert

Good advertising practice

When it comes to advertising you should ideally follow this process:

1 Decide on the objectives of the advertising campaign

- An established business may have decided that it needs to stop a slide in sales or target a particular competitor via comparative advertising.
- For a new business, the objective might be to obtain maximum visibility for the new venture within a particular area. If you are about to go head to head with one major competitor, you might want a comparative advert to explain to potential customers why your product is better.
- Whatever the objective of the campaign, it will drive the following stages.

2 Identify the target audience for the campaign

- This will help concentrate the available budget and resources on the right group of people rather than spreading it too thinly to catch a wider audience.

3 Set the budget

- Particularly in a start-up situation, this is likely to place a significant constraint on how ambitious you can be with your advertising spend. There is no point in proceeding to the next stages of planning unless you know what amount you have available.

4 Devise the correct advertising strategy for reaching that audience

- How is the product or service to be positioned in the market?
- What are the brand values that you wish to communicate?
- Reflect these in the content of the advertising and the choice of media in which the adverts are run.

5 Choose the media in which the advertising will be placed

- This will be possible once you have identified the target audience, set the budget and devised the strategy. You may decide to run the adverts on the radio alone, in a number of local newspapers, in a national newspaper or via the internet.

6 Create and produce the advertisements

- If you are using an agency to create advertising for you, they need to know the results of the above elements so they understand what you are hoping to achieve from your advertising and where it is going to be run. This would all form part of the agency's brief.
- If you are creating the adverts yourself, while there are no hard and fast rules, a useful rule to work with is the AIDA principle (see jargon buster, opposite).

7 Plan and buy media space for the advertisements

- Using the available budget, plan which media your adverts will run in, when they will run and then reserve space to ensure that this happens. For maximum impact, you may need to co-ordinate the advertising with other marketing and promotional activities you are trying.

If you are not engaging an agency or buyer to do it for you, drive a hard bargain with the media – particularly in an economic downturn. While some publications and venues are so successful that they rarely have to discount their rates, many other publications and media would rather have business at a lower rate than none at all. Never accept the rate card at face value. You should, wherever possible, try to haggle. Some publications or channels may have weaker sister publications or channels and offer promotional deals with those.

Legal rules applying to advertising

Advertising is subject to regulation and there are laws that need to be complied with. Some laws can be enforced by state bodies, such as the Office of Fair Trading (OFT) or local Trading Standards departments. Others can be privately enforced under the civil law by the directly affected parties.

Many of these laws and rules overlap. For example, if you run an advertisement comparing your product with the products of a named competitor and your advert denigrates the competitor or the comparison is misleading, you might be doing the following:

- Infringing your competitor's trade mark.
- Breaching consumer protection laws.
- Breaking the Advertising Standards Authority (ASA) Code (see box, below).

In fact, in general, you must be careful about including third-party content in your advertising. For example, you cannot put another person's photograph in your advert just because it has been published in, say, a newspaper or put on the internet.

You must also ensure that your advertising is truthful and does not mislead. If you make claims for your products or services, make sure that you can back them up with robust, objective evidence. Otherwise, you are at risk.

The ASA Code

The laws applicable to advertising can be complicated. Read or download them from the ASA website (see below). As a general rule of thumb, if your advertising complies with the ASA Code, you are unlikely to be in breach of any of the rules and laws referred to here.

The ASA website is www.asa.org.uk. To help you determine whether what you are doing with your advertising is legal, review the chapters in this book dealing with copyright and other IP rights.

Exploiting your IP

You have come up with a great business idea or invention and have protected your IP. How can you exploit it and make money with a minimum of risk? The answer might be to let someone else do the hard work for you. This could mean granting a licence, appointing a distributor or agent or building the business through franchising. This chapter explains more about these concepts and what they involve.

9

Your options

A typical start-up business is unlikely to be able to set up, staff and tool its own new factory to make its products. If you have invented something new or created a design for something, you will probably need to find someone else to make it for you. However, you can go one step further than that and have someone else market and sell the product, too.

For many businesses, the best way to exploit your brand, your product or your invention might be to join up with an established organisation through:

- **Granting a licence to someone** to exploit your IP rights.
- **Appointing a distributor** to promote and sell your goods in a particular territory.
- **Appointing an agent** to sell your goods.
- **Setting up a franchising** arrangement.

《《 You might choose to grant a licence on your product, or appoint a distributor or an agent, or set up a franchising arrangement. **》》**

These are all ways of maximising your potential income stream from a bright idea or protected IP right.

LICENSING

Licensing is where the rights holder (the 'licensor') grants permission to a third party (the 'licensee') to manufacture and/or sell goods or services incorporating or using the patent, trade mark or design in return for licence fees (known as 'royalties'). The royalties are usually paid to the licensor as a percentage of sales.

DISTRIBUTORSHIP

In a distributorship, the rights holder appoints a third party (the 'distributor') to promote and sell his or her goods in an appointed territory. The rights holder sells the goods to the distributor for this purpose and makes its profit from the mark up on the price that is charged to the distributor.

Licensing is explained in full on pages 166–72; distributorships on pages 173–5; agents on pages 176–7, and fanchising on pages 178–9.

AGENCY

Through an agency, the rights holder (known as the 'principal' in this context) appoints an agent (or agents) in a territory to find buyers for the products and to sell them on the principal's behalf. The goods are then supplied by the principal to the customer. The agent is paid a commission on the sales achieved.

FRANCHISING

This occurs when the rights holder ('the franchisor') appoints a third party ('the franchisee') to operate the business in a particular place using common branding, products and operating procedures devised by the franchisor. The franchisor is paid a percentage fee from the turnover of the franchisee.

DECIDING WHICH OPTION IS BEST FOR YOU

Some businesses use a combination of the available options. For example, they may appoint a distributor to sell in the UK, agents to sell in other European countries, a franchise model to help expand in the US and a licensing arrangement to exploit the market in Asia.

In order to determine which option is right for your business, you need to know what each option entails. This chapter looks at them all in detail and sums up on page 180 with a pros and cons table.

❝ Some businesses use a combination of the available options and might have a distributor in the UK, agents to cover Europe, a franchise in the US and a licensing arrangement in Asia. ❞

Licensing

If you are an IP rights owner, you have the option of licensing some or all of those rights to another party. This can be an attractive alternative to trying to do everything yourself.

WHAT IS LICENSING?

A 'licence' is simply a permission granted by the owner to a third party to use the rights as stipulated by the rights owner. Licences can be granted in various forms. For example:

- A copyright licence can be divided into separate licences covering use of the copyright work in broadcast media, in print media and via the internet.
- A trade mark licence involves licensing a third party to manufacture goods bearing the trade mark and then to sell them.

The benefit of licensing someone to use the rights is that the licensor can sit back and earn royalties from the licence of their rights while it is the licensee that does the work, and shoulders the bulk of the risk.

FINDING A SUITABLE LICENSEE

It is important to choose your licensee with care. There is no point in appointing a licensee who is not going to be able to make a success of the licence. If they do not manufacture the product properly or promote it successfully, the value of the

IP rights you have licensed will be diminished – and possibly ruined. Plus you will not earn the licensing income that you want. Do not be blinded simply by being offered large sums of money. If the licensee can't actually pay those sums, you are wasting your time.

Before appointing anyone as your licensee, you should therefore ask as many questions as you can in your discussions with them to try to establish whether they have the necessary attributes to make a success of any licence.

Besides the information you gather from a potential licnesee, you should also carry out some basic independent background checks of your own. For example, if you are doing business with a large, well-known company, you may need to do minimal research to establish their credentials. But if the company is based overseas or is neither a public company nor an established one, consider obtaining a company report on them. You will want to establish some basic information about them, such as:

- How long have they been in business?
- Are they an incorporated company, a partnership, a publicly quoted

company? The type of business that they are might affect their attitude to risk or likely ability to pay debts if they go bust.

- In which countries do they have offices, factories or some other kind of presence?
- How big are they in terms of turnover and employees?
- What do their most recent accounts look like and what is their financial track record?
- Are there any stories (especially adverse stories) about them published on the internet?
- What other products are they already manufacturing or selling and do they have any other licences, such as for a household name brand or for competing products?

Financial history

You must also establish the company's credit rating and accounting history. Use companies such as Dun & Bradstreet, Experion and Equifax (see below) who, in return for a fee, will supply you with a report covering such matters.

If you use a reputable company, they will give you a reasonably good idea of the financial health of the subject. They will include details such as whether there are any court judgments outstanding (a sure sign of financial difficulty) and they

can give an indication of where the subject is compared to its peers in terms of likelihood of business failure. However, they might not be fully up to date and you will have to pay a fee. For UK companies, you can obtain copies of accounts filed at Companies House very much more cheaply (a few pounds

| Case Study | Sarah and Tim |

Sarah and Tim have designed a stylish new baby buggy. They have invested a lot of money in patenting their unique new folding mechanism for the buggy. They have also protected the appearance of the buggy by means of a Community design registration. But they do not have the means to raise finance to have their product manufactured and have yet to think up a brand name for it.

They decide to grant an exclusive licence to a US company to make and sell their buggies in return for paying them an 8 per cent royalty on sales. They and the manufacturer are going to devise a name for the buggy, which will be trade marked and that trade mark will appear on the product, but Sarah and Tim will retain ownership of the trade mark.

Sarah and Tim have carried out some checks on the manufacturer and are satisfied that it has the resources and track record to make a success of the new venture. The next step is for them to negotiate the basic terms on which the licence will be granted (see the continuation of this case study on page 169).

The websites for credit rating companies are: www.dnb.co.uk (Dun & Bradstreet), www.experion.co.uk (Experion) and www.Equifax.co.uk (Equifax).

compared to £70–£100 for some credit agencies) although the information has no analysis or commentary and it won't be completely up to date.

> **"There are many pitfalls for rights holders that can have disastrous consequences. "**

THE KEY TERMS TO INCLUDE IN A LICENCE

The basic premise of a licence is to allow a third party to use your IP rights in return for paying you a royalty for the privilege. There are a number of basic points that will apply to every licence and some more specialised matters that will depend on the nature of the rights you are licensing and the scope of what you are allowing the licensee to do.

If you are about to enter into a binding agreement to licence your valuable IP rights, you should, if at all possible, seek legal advice to guide you through the process of negotiating the agreement. There are many pitfalls for rights holders, which can have disastrous consequences if they are not covered in the agreement.

Jargon buster

Exclusive licence A contract under which the licensee is given the exclusive rights under the licence in a territory to the exclusion of everyone else – including the rights holder
Non-exclusive licence Where the rights holder reserves the right to appoint more than one licensee in a territory, including selling there itself
Royalty-free licence A licence where no royalties are payable by the licensee
Sole licence A licence where the licensor has granted only one licence
Sub-licensing of rights Where a licensee is appointed, that licensee may itself grant a sub-licence to another party to do certain things with the IP rights in order for the licensee to fulfil its obligations under its licence. To ensure the licensee does not breach its agreement with the licensor, the obligations imposed on the sub-licensee should normally mirror the obligations in the main licence

Most licences will contain a lot of detailed terms and conditions, but before you reach the stage of getting into such detail, you will need to reach an agreement with the potential licensee

The website of the World Intellectual Property Organisation (WIPO) contains links to many useful articles about licensing. Go to www.wipo.int.

in relation to the key points. These would be as follows:

- What rights are being licensed – trade marks, patents, designs?
- What is the scope of the licence – will it cover manufacture and sale of products or just manufacture?
- What territory will the licence apply to – just the UK, the EU, the world or specific countries?
- Is the licence to be 'exclusive', 'sole' or 'non-exclusive'?

- What royalties will be payable by the licensee?
- What is the duration (term) of the licence?
- Will any sub-licensing of rights be permitted?

❝You must agree on what rights are being licensed, and in what territories.❞

Case Study Sarah and Tim (continued)

Sarah and Tim have reached agreement with their licensee on the main points of a deal but subject to the precise terms of the licence agreement that has yet to be drafted and agreed. They draw up a deal sheet confirming the agreed terms as follows:

Deal terms – subject to contract

Licensed property: European Patents Nos 40XXY34 & 68XX98Y and Community design nos 0005XX88.001-0005XX88.12.

Scope: Manufacture, promotion and sale of baby buggy incorporating the licensed property.

Exclusivity: Exclusive licence.

Territory: Worldwide.

Term: 5 years (option to renew for 3 more years).

Royalty: Up-front fee of £50,000 plus 8% royalty of net sales.

Buggy name: To be registered in Sarah and Tim's names and licensed on a royalty-free basis to the manufacturer for the duration of the licence.

The words 'subject to contract' are important. This means that the deal agreed between the parties is not yet binding on them (rather like if in England you accept a verbal offer to buy your house). Sarah and Tim's 'subject to contract' deal will only be completed and enforceable as a contract once the contract itself has been negotiated and signed off.

THE LICENCE AGREEMENT

Having reached agreement on the main terms of the deal, the next step is to come up with a proper written licence agreement that incorporates the main points. The agreement will also need to contain specific provisions to ensure the proper working of the licence in practice and to protect the parties' rights.

Your priority as licensor is to ensure that the licence agreement works as strongly as possible in your favour. The agreement should also spell things out clearly so there is no ambiguity about what is meant by the key terms and expressions used in it.

For example, in the Sarah and Tim case study on page 169, it has been agreed that they will receive a £50,000 fee and that royalties will be paid at the rate of '8% of sales'. The agreement needs to specify the exact details of this. The following questions need to be addressed in the wording of the agreement:

- **The £50,000 fee:** when is it payable? Would this be on the date of signing the agreement or within a fixed period of time, such as 14 days, of signing it?
- **What happens to the initial fee** if there is a breach of the agreement and the licensor wishes to terminate it early? What happens if the licensee fails to generate enough sales to earn sufficient royalties? The agreement needs to stipulate whether the £50,000 is a non-refundable fee paid irrespective of such events or whether

it is recoupable against royalties, in which case no royalties would be payable until they exceed £50,000.

- **What is meant by 'sales'?** Are these 'gross sales' or 'net sales' and, if so, how are such sales calculated? What items are deducted to arrive at net sales?
- **When are royalties paid** – quarterly, monthly or annually?
- **Are there to be minimum royalty figures** that the licensee must achieve and, if so, what are they and what happens if they are not met?
- **What safeguards does the licensor have** for checking that royalties are being properly calculated and accounted for?

A typical licence agreement must cover this kind of detail – and that's for each aspect, not just the fee and royalties. As well as the main obligations and royalty provisions, there are many practical points that need to be covered in the licence agreement. For example:

- **If you are licensing the manufacture of goods,** you will want the licensee to take out insurance against claims for faulty products or for where products might cause personal injuries. You would also want an indemnity from the licensee against claims arising from the licensee's default.

- If the licence goes beyond manufacturing and includes sales, you will want to ensure that you, as the licensor, are able to approve advertisements and marketing materials that are put out relating to the products. You do not want them adopting a strategy that conflicts with how you see the brand or product developing.

- If a trade mark is involved, you need to make sure the licensee puts your mark on the products being made and sells them in the way you want and do not themselves register trade marks that are the same or similar to yours. It is important to ensure that the licensee agrees not to do anything that would affect the IP rights being licensed.

Licensing: a checklist

A licence would normally contain details of the following:

1 The identity of the parties.
2 A good definitions section listing various 'defined terms' used in the agreement.
3 Whether the licence is exclusive or not.
4 What the licence is for.
5 The duration of the licence and any renewal provisions.
6 Obligations of the parties.
7 Royalties.
8 Quality control and approval.
9 Licensor's right of access to licensee's accounts and sales records.
10 Marketing, advertising and promotion.
11 Goodwill and title to IP rights.
12 Confidentiality.
13 Insurance.
14 Taxes.
15 Whether sub-licensing or assignment is allowed.
16 Termination provisions.
17 How to deal with infringements.
18 Indemnities and warranties.
19 'Boilerplate' clauses.
20 Jurisdiction.

Jargon buster

Assignment Where a party transfers its ownership and title to something to another party

Boilerplate The term given to various 'standard' clauses in a contract, which are usually present regardless of what the contract is for. This could be a clause stipulating where notices under the contract have to be served or stating which country's law applies to the contract

Confidentiality Contracts may have clauses imposing confidentiality restrictions that limit what the parties can reveal to third parties about the contract, its contents or the subject matter of the contract

Goodwill When a business trades, it builds up a goodwill and reputation in the market. This goodwill is a valuable, but intangible part of a business's value

Jurisdiction The right of the courts of a particular country to try cases

Title to IP rights The ownership of IP rights

Obviously, there are variations on licences, depending on the nature of what is being licensed and what its scope is, such as manufacturing only, or manufacture and sale. It is beyond the scope of this book to list all the specifics relating to each, but the checklist on the previous page contains an outline of what most licences should contain.

'KNOW-HOW' LICENCES

Trade marks, patents designs and copyright are all types of IP rights that can be licensed by the rights holder. But there are some things that do not fall within the scope of any of those rights.

Sometimes, a party will have information (or 'know-how') that is not, in itself, susceptible to protection as a design, copyright work, patent or trade mark, but yet is valuable. For example, it might be a recipe for a drink or it might be a detailed set of instructions for performing certain tasks in a business in a particular sequence that makes them more efficient than if they were performed a different way.

Such matters may be protected by the law of confidential information and a confidentiality agreement (see the NDA on pages 28–31). Where such information is confidential, another party can nevertheless be licensed to use it on the basis that it keeps the matters confidential.

The problem is that such know-how may be something that can readily be copied once it is put into practice in the public domain. You should therefore think carefully about whether there is anything you are giving to your licensee that could be subjected to such a 'know-how' licence as part of the overall licence agreement.

> **❝ Know-how may be protected by the law of confidential information. ❞**

Distributorships

If you are able to have your goods manufactured, you still may not have a ready route to market for them. Appointing a distributor may be the answer. Distributors buy the goods from you and then take responsibility for promoting and selling them in the territory where they operate.

With a distributorship arrangement, you make money from the margin between the cost of the goods to you and the price you obtain from your distributor. Once the goods are sold to your distributor, it is they who bear the bulk of the commercial risk. They have to sell the stock and promote and market the products. If they fail to sell the goods, they bear the loss.

DISTRIBUTOR BENEFITS

If you have not chosen the licensing route or set up a franchise, you will have to promote and sell your products yourself, appoint sales agents or appoint a distributor.

The benefit of choosing a distributor is that it means the business of promoting and selling your products is being done by a third party, rather than you. You will not have to incur the burden of administration, advertising costs and hiring employees to go around selling. The distributor will be responsible for selling to multiple outlets and collecting its debts. You will have only one company to deal with.

Provided you put in place a proper distributorship agreement, you can also ensure the goodwill built up in your trade

| Case Study | Toby |

Toby has a Community trade mark for his luxury organic soap brand. The brand has started to generate significant sales via the internet. A German cosmetics distributor approaches Toby and asks if it can distribute the product in return for the exclusive distribution rights in Germany.

Toby has no knowledge of the German market and no office there. Appointing a well-established company that already has a distribution network in place is an ideal way for him to generate sales in that market. His Community trade mark means that he is in a position to give his new distributor an advantage by being the only official distributor of goods bearing that trade mark.

mark or brand remains with you so that at the end of the distributorship term, if you decide not to re-appoint the distributor, you will reap the benefit. Unlike with, say, commercial agents, there are no laws that require you to pay compensation to a distributor once its appointment has ended.

CHOOSING YOUR DISTRIBUTOR

To choose a distributor, you should carry out the same kinds of research as when choosing a licensee (see pages 166–8).

THE DISTRIBUTORSHIP AGREEMENT

As with licensing, it is strongly advisable that you take legal advice before appointing a distributor since there are plenty of potential pitfalls.

Many of the terms applicable to a licence agreement would be equally apt for a distributorship arrangement (see the box, below). But some specific issues you need to think about are:

- **Terms of sale.** Because you are selling goods to your distributor, you will need to have terms and conditions of sale that govern the supply of those goods. These will incorporate such things as payment terms, delivery arrangements, documentation to be provided, retention of title in the event of non-payment and returns. It is common for the distributorship agreement to incorporate a separate set of standard terms and conditions.
- **Marketing, sales and promotion.** In return for the distributorship rights, you will want the distributor to take responsibility for promoting and marketing the products in its allocated territory. So the agreement should contain provisions stipulating minimum

Jargon buster

Exclusive distributor A contract under which the distributor is given the exclusive rights under the distributorship in a territory to the exclusion of everyone else – including the rights holder

Non-exclusive distributor Where the rights holder reserves the right to appoint more than one distributor in a territory, including selling there itself

Selective distribution For some premium-type goods it may be desirable to restrict the number of outlets that can sell them to those who meet certain quality criteria. A network of such distributors is known as a 'selective distribution system'

Sole distributor Where the rights holder agrees to appoint only one distributor in a territory, but reserves its own right to sell goods in that territory too

❝ Take legal advice before appointing a distributor. ❞

Distributorship: a checklist

You can essentially use the licensing checklist on page 171 by substituting the term 'distributorship' for the word 'licence' and by making the following changes to it:

- In place of item 7 'royalties', substitute 'prices and payment'.
- In place of item 8 'quality control and approval', substitute 'conditions of sale'.

sums that must be spent by the distributor on such activities.

- **Minimum sales.** You will want your distributor to have an incentive to promote your products. Setting minimum sales targets linked to the continuation of the distributorship will provide an incentive, but at the same time give you the option to terminate the arrangement if it isn't working out.

COMPETITION LAWS

Appointing distributors can bring into play EU and domestic competition laws. These are laws aimed at preventing unfair practices and anti-competitive conduct.

You will have heard of cases where the authorities have punished well-known companies for anti-competitive conduct. For example, British Airways was penalised in 2008 for such conduct in relation to fuel surcharges after the company was found to have agreed with other airlines to set the price of such surcharges. Likewise, a number of sports retailers and brands were fined in 2007 for fixing prices for replica football kits so as to keep prices at a certain level to the detriment of consumers.

Competition law tends to bite where the businesses concerned have a sufficient size and/or market share so they are significant enough to have an appreciable effect on trade within the UK or between EU states or else abuse a

Guaranteeing payment

Ensuring you are paid for the goods supplied to the distributor is essential. If dealing with an overseas distributor, consider using a letter of credit to guarantee payment if you cannot secure payment in advance.

dominant position. This is unlikely to be the case with a start-up or small business in its initial stages. However, it is a good idea to avoid practices that could, in time, conflict with competition laws. Examples of actions that could, in some circumstances, fall foul of competition law and which should be avoided are as follows:

- **Attempting to fix prices,** such as requiring your distributor to adopt a minimum price for goods bearing your trade mark or fixing minimum resale prices.
- **Placing territorial restrictions** on resale of products.

> ! The consequences of falling foul of competition law can be serious. It could render your agreement null and void, expose you to legal action or even criminal penalties. Take legal advice.

 For more information about competition laws, go to the OFT's website at www.oft.gov.uk.

Agents

Another way of building sales and penetrating markets with outside help is to use agents to sell your products. Before you consider using an agency, read this section to find out what you should expect from the relationship.

USING AN AGENT

Working with an agent involves supplying each one with pricing, promotional literature and perhaps training in aspects of the products. They can then go out into their sales 'territory' and promote or sell the products. The orders they obtain are met by you and it is you, not the agent, who is responsible for supplying the goods. The agent will receive a sales commission usually based on the sales they achieve.

There are a number of reasons why you might prefer to appoint agents rather than distributors:

- **You have more contact** with your end-customers.
- **You exert more control** over prices and how your products are advertised and marketed.
- **You have considerably more freedom** to control your choice of customers.

- In the early stages of launching a new **business** you may find it hard to find a distributor to assume the risks and burdens of a distributorship.
- **As the business grows,** there are generally fewer competition law issues that apply to agency relationships.

> **❝An agent will promote or sell the products in their territory, but you are responsible for supplying the goods.❞**

 To read the contents of the Commercial Agents Regulations 1993, go to the Office of Public Sector Information (OPSI) at www.opsi.gov.uk/si/si1993/Uksi_19933053_en_1.htm.

The Commercial Agents Regulations

Unfortunately, a piece of EU legislation – the Commercial Agents Regulations 1993 (as amended) – has made it more complicated to appoint an agent in the European Economic Area (EEA). These regulations have introduced mandatory rights for agents and, in particular, rights that apply on the termination of the agency arrangement. These can have the effect of leaving the rights holder (you!) with a nasty bill for compensation if an agent is dispensed with. The compensation provisions cannot be contracted out of, but correct drafting of an agency agreement can limit their impact.

The regulations do not apply where the agency is concerned solely with negotiating the sale or purchase of 'services' as opposed to 'goods'. The Regulations can give rise to considerable complications so, if at all possible, take legal advice before appointing an agent so that you can be as clear as possible about the potential costs that could arise on termination of the agency and any other aspects of the regulations that apply to your business.

« If you dispense with an agent in the EEA, you could be left with a nasty bill for compensation. »

Using an agency: a checklist

You can essentially use the licensing checklist on page 171 by substituting the term 'agency' for the words 'licence' or 'licensing' and 'principal' for the word 'licensor' and by making the following changes to the list:

- In place of item 7 'royalties', substitute 'commission and payment'.
- Item 8 'quality control and approval' is unnecessary.
- Item 16 is very important. These provisions should provide for the agent to have an 'indemnity' on termination of the agency, rather than being able to seek compensation under the Commercial Agents Regulations (see above).

Franchising

Most people will have heard of brands such as Dyno-Rod, MacDonalds, Snappy Snaps, Domino's Pizzas and Toni&Guy. These are just some of the businesses that use franchising as a business model to help sustain and grow their business.

WHAT IS FRANCHISING?

Franchising involves a 'franchisor' licensing a 'franchisee' to operate a business using the franchisor's branding, trade marks and benefiting from a package of support from the franchisor. The idea is that it benefits both sides.

The franchisee can run their own business, but without having to start from scratch and reduce the level of risk that comes with a typical business start-up.

They are able to trade under the franchisor's brand name and benefit from any goodwill and reputation that has already been established for that brand. They also usually benefit from training help and assistance from the franchisor to help get started and once the franchise is in operation, they receive further support. This could involve benefiting from the franchisor's buying power to source materials at a discount to the market.

For the franchisor, franchising can be a good way of building their brand and, again, minimising risk, capital outlay and liabilities. In return for a one-off up-front fee, they help the franchisee establish the business and then draw income from the franchise over its term in the form of a franchising fee. They may also derive income from the mark-up on materials, such as stationary and other branded items, supplied to the franchisee.

FRANCHISING AND A NEW BUSINESS

Franchising works best when the franchisor has already established a brand reputation by successful trading in a relevant territory. The attraction to the would-be franchisee of taking a franchise is likely to be greater in such cases than if the franchisor has no track record and, as yet, no brand reputation. After all, one of the main attractions for a franchisee of taking a franchise is the fact that it combines an opportunity to run your own business, but with the comfort of doing so under an established brand and using a proven business model. But if the right kind of business is being launched, it could still be a potential option for a new business.

SETTING UP A FRANCHISED BUSINESS

If you are going to adopt franchising as your preferred business model, two things are essential: a properly drafted franchise agreement and a suitable franchising manual.

The agreement

This is vital so that you can exert the necessary degree of control over the way each franchisee conducts their business. They will be using your trading name and will be viewed by the outside world as being your business. So they must create a good impression on customers and use your brand in a way that fits with how you want it presented.

The franchise agreement must include suitable restrictions aimed at stopping the franchisee from operating a competing business during the life of the franchise agreement. On termination, the

 Do not attempt to draft the franchise agreement yourself. It would be a false economy. Besides which, once you have your franchise agreement, you will be able to re-use it each time you appoint a new franchisee. You would be strongly advised to have a solicitor draw up a suitable franchising agreement for you.

franchisee should then be required to deliver up all copies of the manual, stationary and other materials bearing the trade marks and details of customers and leads.

The operating manual

An operating manual sets out operating procedures and rules for conducting the franchised business – such as uniforms to be worn by staff, standards of hygiene, arrangement of premises and signage – and the use of trade marks.

If you are starting your business from scratch, it may be difficult to draft a suitably comprehensive and practical manual because you will not have experience of operating the business. Ideally, you should operate a pilot project as a 'test bed' for the franchising scheme. In this way, it would be possible to revise the manual with the benefit of some actual operational experience.

 For more information about franchising, go to the British Franchising Association website at www.thebfa.org. The BFA is the governing body of franchising and the website offers help and advice together with up-to-date news and events.

The pros and cons of contracting out work

Licensing

Pros
- Offloads risk onto licensee in return for royalties.
- Reduces capital and other costs that have to be incurred by you to take the products or services to market.

Cons
- Loss of some control over the whole process.
- You may become dependent upon the licensee.

Distributorship

Pros
- Offloads risk of selling goods onto the distributor.
- You have no liability for acts of the distributor (in contrast with those of agent).
- With a sole or exclusive distributorship, you deal with only one company not a plethora of different customers.
- A distributor has no right to compensation or indemnity payment on termination of the distributorship.

Cons
- Danger of putting all your eggs in one basket by appointing a sole or exclusive distributor – if anything goes wrong.
- Potentially more issues with UK and EU competition law than with agency arrangement.
- Reduces direct contact between rights holder and the end customer/consumer.
- Margins might be lower than with licence or agency arrangement.

Using an agent

Pros
- Agent may take less in commission than a distributor takes by way of margin.
- You have more control over pricing and marketing and promotion of your goods.
- You have more direct contact with the customer.
- You have more choice as to who you contract, with fewer competition law problems.

Cons
- Compensation or indemnity is payable to agent upon termination of the agency agreement.
- Using an agent overseas may lead to taxation issues if you are treated as having a trading presence in the territory.
- Commercial Agents Regulations still uncertain in scope and effect (see page 177).

Franchising

Pros
- Offloads much of the risk and costs of running a business onto a third party.
- Enables rapid growth of business at relatively low cost since franchisees pick up most of the bills and provide their own capital to help with expansion.
- Franchisees are highly motivated to succeed.

Cons
- May not be so easy to set up where the business is new.
- More difficult to attract potential franchisees prior to the business becoming better known.
- Loss of direct control – even if a good agreement is in place, on a day-to-day basis, the franchisee effectively runs the show.

Infringements

Once you have acquired your IP rights, you need to protect them otherwise they can be a waste of money. Unfortunately, as an IP rights owner you are likely, sooner or later, to encounter someone else infringing your rights. This chapter will help you deal with such infringements.

Infringement actions

Where a party is infringing your rights, the ultimate way in which the infringer is dealt with if they will not stop is by means of legal proceedings. This involves issuing a claim and pursuing litigation, possibly to a full trial.

For many small businesses, however, it simply isn't an option to pursue cases all the way to trial because of the expense. So in this chapter, the focus is primarily on what you can do before you have to take the drastic step of issuing legal proceedings.

REMEDIES AVAILABLE IN INFRINGEMENT ACTIONS

The potential remedies that can be imposed by the court in cases where IP rights are infringed are essentially the same, regardless of the type of IP right involved. These include:

- An injunction prohibiting further infringing acts or requiring the infringer to do certain things, such as disclose information or deliver up infringing items.
- An award of damages or an account of the profits made by the infringer.
- An order that the infringer pay a proportion of the rights holder's legal costs.
- Publication of the judgment at the infringer's expense.

When legal action is started, it may be several months (sometimes over a year)

Jargon buster

Account of profits Instead of damages, the court can require an infringer to pay over a sum in respect of the profits made from the infringing activity

Damages A sum of money the court awards to the successful claimant to compensate him for losses caused by infringements of his rights by the defendant

Injunction An order of the court requiring the party concerned to either do or refrain from doing a particular act. Breach of an injunction is a serious matter and is a contempt of court punishable by imprisonment, a fine or both

Interim injunction An injunction imposed by the court to protect a party's rights in the period before the case can be finally heard and decided at trial. Again, breach of such an injunction by the party injuncted (or even a third party) is a contempt of court

before it will come to trial. In particularly urgent cases, where intervention from the court is needed in the meantime, it may be possible to obtain an **interim injunction** to prevent further infringements or to ensure that infringing items are not disposed of.

HOW ARE IP RIGHTS INFRINGED?

Different laws and regulations apply to different types of IP rights. The first thing you need to be able to do is to recognise an infringement when you see one.

In each of the chapters dealing with patents, trade marks, designs and copyright, you will have seen what each right legally gives you. For example, having a registered trade mark, broadly speaking, gives you the right to prevent anyone else from using the same or a similar sign in relation to identical or similar goods. So if you notice a competitor using a sign that is confusingly close to your own trade mark, you may have an infringement on your hands.

With copyright, you have the right to stop someone using the whole or a substantial part of your copyright work without your permission, whether by copying it or dealing with it. For example, if you notice that someone is using photographs on their website that you took for your own website, you will know that they are infringing your copyright.

The table overleaf summarises the principal acts that can infringe the different types of IP rights.

BEFORE YOU DO ANYTHING

If you think you have come across an infringement, try to avoid a knee jerk reaction. Look at what is happening and consider the situation carefully.

The first thing you need to do is to gather some tangible evidence of the offending activity. In that way, you will have something to back up your claim, whether you deal with it yourself or instruct a lawyer.

Suppose you discover someone is selling products incorporating your patented invention or which are made to your protected design? If possible, you need to:

- Obtain a **physical sample** of the infringing product so that you can see it for yourself. Photographs can mislead.
- **Get proof of who is selling it.**
- Obtain a **copy of the advertisement,** if the seller is advertising it.

When putting together your evidence, it is useful, if possible, to have the dates of the offending activity since, depending on the particular scenario, this could be important to proving the claim. Remember that in the internet age, a website can be altered in minutes, so if you see something on the internet one day, it may not be there the next day – try to capture a copy of the offending activity on the web there and then.

Gathering evidence is largely a matter of common sense. Think of yourself as the judge. If you were hearing the case,

Acts of infringement

IP right	Infringing act
Patent (see pages 21–44)	• Where the invention is a product: making, disposing of, offering to dispose of, using, importing or keeping the product for disposal or otherwise. • Where the invention is a process: using the process or offering it for use in the UK when the party knows, or it is obvious to a reasonable person that its use in the UK without permission would be an infringement. • Where the invention is a process: disposing of, offering to dispose of, using or importing any product obtained directly by means of that process or keeping it for disposal or otherwise. • Offering without permission any of the means relating to an essential element of the invention, for putting the invention into effect when the party knows or it is obvious that those means are suitable and intended for use in putting the invention into effect in the UK.
Copyright (see pages 45–62)	• Without the permission of the copyright owner: copying, lending or renting, distributing to the public, adapting, showing or playing in public, communicating the to the public, copies of the whole or a substantial part of the copyright work (or authorising the doing of any such acts). • Importing, possessing in the course of business, selling, letting or offering for sale, distributing privately but excessively an article that the party knows or has reason to believe is an infringing copy of the work. • Falsely attributing authorship of a work.
Registered trade mark (see pages 63-88)	• Using an identical sign to the trade mark in relation to identical goods or services to those for which the mark is registered. • Using an identical sign to the trade mark in relation to similar goods or services or a similar sign in relation to identical or similar goods or services where there is a likelihood of confusion. • Only where the trade mark has a 'reputation': using an identical or similar sign in relation to goods or services where the use is without due cause and takes unfair advantage of the trade mark or is detrimental to its distinctive character or repute.

IP right	Infringing act
Passing off (see pages 76-7)	• Making a misrepresentation to consumers or the trade that the goods or services in question are those of, or licensed by, the rights holder when they are not. • A misrepresentation that the defendant is part of the rights owner's business or associated with it when they are not. • A misrepresentation by the defendant that it or its products or services are endorsed or recommended by the rights holder when, in fact, they are not.
Designs (see pages 89-108)	• UK and Community registered designs: making, offering, putting on the market, importing, exporting or using a product in which the design is incorporated or to which it is applied or stocking such a product. This only applies where the offending product or offending part of it produces on the informed user a different overall impression to the protected design. • Community unregistered designs: as above, provided the offending product or part was copied from the protected design. • UK unregistered designs: copying the protected design by producing articles exactly or substantially to the design; and/or importing into the UK for commercial purposes or having in possession for commercial purposes or selling, hiring, or offering for sale an article that the party knows or has reason to believe is an infringing article.

❝ This table summarises the principal acts that can infringe the different types of IP rights. ❞

Case Study: John

John has been running a business providing landscape gardening services and uses a website to help promote his business. On the website in his 'gallery' he displays photographs of completed projects.

One day he notices that a competitor has opened a similar business and is using photographs from John's own portfolio to promote their business via the internet.

John makes screen grabs of all the pages of the website where the offending photographs are displayed and emails them to himself as attachments so he has a date record of when he gathered the evidence. He then asks a friend to call the infringers for a quote and obtains a copy of their promotional literature, which again contains copies of some of his photographs.

He now has proof that they are infringing his copyright (as well as passing off his work as theirs).

what factual evidence would you need to see to prove that the activity in question had occurred?

IS IT REALLY AN INFRINGEMENT?

When you have finished gathering your evidence, you may still have doubts about the merits of your case. Many IP cases are not straightforward. You need to consider the possible defences that the infringer may have to justify its activity or to defend any claim.

In trade mark cases, for example, one of the most common defences arises where the trade mark is being used purely descriptively (see the case study, left), or it may be being used in comparative advertising in which a competitor compares its own products or prices with those of the trade mark owner.

In cases where you are uncertain, this could be the moment to seek professional advice from a solicitor. You do not want to risk being sued for making 'unjustified threats' of infringement proceedings. Nor do you want to risk becoming embroiled in a court battle that you might well lose.

Case Study: Wet Wet Wet

The rock group Wet Wet Wet registered their name as a trade mark for a variety of goods and services, including in relation to books and printed matter. A third party published a book about the group under the title *Wet Wet Wet* – identical to the trade mark registered by the group. The group sued for trade mark infringement. Surely an open and shut case, you would think.

But no. The court held that there was no trade mark infringement. It is a defence for a person to use a trade mark to describe the characteristics of their goods – provided that use is in accordance with honest practices. The book was a book about the group Wet Wet Wet, so calling it by that name was not infringement. The use was descriptive and honest.

Bringing such a claim is not to be done lightly. The costs of such litigation are substantial. If you have a solicitor representing you, then, unless you have agreed a **'no win, no fee'** arrangement, you will probably have to pay his or her costs whatever happens. If you win your case, you may end up recovering a proportion of those costs from the loser. However, if you lose your case, you may be liable for paying part of the other party's costs – plus your own.

In many IP infringement disputes, the number one priority is to ensure that the infringements stop and that, if possible, some or all of the legal costs spent on pursuing the matter can be recovered. There may not be a large damages payout.

So before you embark on what can be an expensive course of action, you need

 You cannot bring legal proceedings for infringement until your patent or other IP right is actually granted. But once you have the patent, you can sue for damages for the period between the publication of your application and the grant – but you need to be careful not to make an 'unjustified threat' of proceedings (see pages 192–4).

to ask yourself what it is that you really want to achieve by taking on the infringer. Would you be content if you succeeded in having them stop the infringements or is it financial compensation that is your priority? If you know what your priorities are, you can shape your legal campaign accordingly.

Jargon buster

No win, no fee Although more common in personal injury litigation, in some IP cases, lawyers may be prepared to act on a no win, no fee basis. This means that if you lose the case, you do not have to pay your own lawyer's legal bill (although you might still be liable to pay part of the winner's legal costs unless you had insured against them). In a no win, no fee case, if you win your case, your lawyer will normally charge significantly more than if you had been on an ordinary retainer

&& The top priority is to stop the infringements from continuing. &&

Resolving disputes

If you are sure that your rights are being infringed and you do not have the funds to instruct a solicitor or prefer to try to resolve the matter yourself first, the next stage is to write a letter to the offending party. This is called a 'letter before action' or a 'demand letter'.

WRITING A DEMAND LETTER

A good letter can go a long way in an IP dispute. It is amazing how many IP owners (even those using professional advisers) do not take sufficient time and trouble to prepare a good letter from the outset. A well-constructed and well-argued letter at this stage can make a decisive contribution to resolving the dispute. By contrast, a poor letter can have the opposite effect or worse, send the wrong signals to the infringer.

A demand letter essentially performs three functions:

- It is your chance to warn the other party that it is infringing your rights and to hopefully persuade them why they should desist rather than incur the expensive and unpleasant consequences of continuing to do so.
- Even if they do not comply with your demand, if nothing else it may flush out how they intend to defend any claim you may bring.
- Except in special cases where you cannot afford to tip off the offender in advance of your intentions (for example, if you need to obtain an injunction to freeze his assets), the letter can be used later to show the court that you gave the other side the chance to stop and only resorted to legal action as a last resort.

❝ A well-constructed and properly argued letter early on can make a decisive contribution. ❞

You must consider your position carefully before you threaten anybody. If you are unsure about your rights, take advice from a solicitor. This book can only be a basic guide to the problem. There are nuances and technical points that only a qualified professional will be familiar with.

Writing a demand letter

Outlined below is the ideal content of a demand letter. A sample is then given overleaf.

1 Explain who you (or your business) are and what your business does.

2 Briefly mention any special attributes your business has, referring, for example to awards and plaudits achieved.

3 Describe and identify the IP rights you will be relying upon:

Patents: briefly summarise what the patented invention is, state whether it is a UK or European patent and give the registration number.

Trade marks: state whether the mark is a UK or Community trade mark, identify the mark itself, give the classes in which it is registered and summarise the part of the specification(s) most relevant to the claim.

Passing off: describe how your business has built up goodwill and reputation by reference to the relevant identifying name, logo, get up or other identification.

Copyright: describe who created the work, when it was created and how you or your business came to have title to it and state what type of copyright work it is, such as literary or artistic.

Unregistered designs: describe what the design is, who created it and when it was first disclosed to the public, how you or your business came to acquire title to it, what products it has been applied to.

Registered designs: describe what the design is, whether it is a UK or Community registered design and give the registration number.

Confidential information: identify what the information or know-how relates to the information you are concerned about and why it is confidential.

4 Describe the facts of what the infringing party has done that amount to infringement of the IP right in question.

5 Confirm the type of infringement alleged.

6 Summarise the consequences of infringement, such as injunction or damages.

7 State what action the infringer needs to take in order to avoid legal action.

8 Set a deadline for a response to your letter.

An example of a demand letter

Dear Sirs

Infringement of Which? trade mark

We are Which? Ltd, part of the well-known Consumer's organisation.

We have been operating in the United Kingdom under the 'Which?' name for over 50 years. Our business is aimed at promoting the interests of consumers through a variety of activities including lobbying, research, testing and comparing consumer products and services and campaigning. We also have extensive publishing activities including via the internet, books and magazines.

Our books are prominently branded with the Which? name and logo.

As a result of successful trading activities over the past 50 years in the UK, we have built up a substantial goodwill and reputation by reference to the Which? brand.

We are writing to you about a serious matter. It concerns the infringement by you of our valuable intellectual property rights.

Our rights

We are the registered proprietor of the UK trade mark registration No. 2356518 for WHICH? in various classes, including for printed matter and publications.

As we have said, because of our long trading history, the Which? brand is very well known to consumers. Consequently, where they see a book bearing the Which? brand, they will believe that the book has been published by us, or with our licence or endorsement.

Your activities

We are aware that you have been advertising for sale a forthcoming range of books that you intend to sell under the brand 'WHICH? publishing'. You say you will be putting these on sale in one month's time but have yet to sell any.

Trade mark infringement and passing off

If you do that, you will be using an identical sign (i.e. 'Which?') in relation to the promotion of identical goods (books) to those for which our trade mark is registered. This amounts to trade mark infringement contrary to the Trade marks Act 1994. You are also taking unfair advantage of our trade mark because of the well-known reputation that the Which? brand has in the minds of consumers. This is also trade mark infringement.

You are also committing passing off because consumers will be confused into thinking that we have published or licensed you to publish books under the Which? name. That is not, of course, correct.

Consequences

As a result of this infringing activity, we are entitled to seek appropriate relief against you, including an injunction to stop you from publishing or promoting any books under that name. We will also be entitled to claim damages or an account of profits arising from your activities if you have started them already.

What you need to do now

You must immediately stop any further use of the sign Which? to promote your business. We require you to undertake in writing that (whether acting via your directors, agents or otherwise) you will immediately and permanently:

1. Cease and desist from infringing our trade mark (whether by advertising, selling or supplying books bearing the sign 'Which?' or any confusingly similar sign in the UK or by any other means)

2. Pay us the sum of £500 by way of a contribution to our costs of enforcing our rights.

If we do not hear from you with a satisfactory response by 5.30pm on [a date 10–14 days in the future would not be unreasonable], we will issue legal proceedings against you in the High Court including seeking the appropriate High Court injunction.

Yours faithfully,

THE PROBLEM OF 'UNJUSTIFIED THREATS'

So far, so good. You have identified that infringing activity is occurring, considered whether there is any justification for it, gathered your evidence and you have prepared a demand letter. However, before you send the demand letter, there is something else you need to think about.

With the exception of cases involving purely passing off or copyright infringement, there is a nasty trap for the would-be IP rights enforcer in the UK, for within the UK legislation that governs patents, registered trade marks and designs are provisions that entitle a party 'aggrieved' by threats of IP infringement proceedings to bring a claim of their own against the person that is making those threats.

Under these rules, if the claim in question proves to be unjustified because there is, in fact, no infringement or if the IP right relied upon is found to be invalid, then the 'aggrieved person' can turn the tables on the rights owner. It is important in this context to realise that the 'aggrieved person' does not have to be the party who actually received the threat. It is enough that they have cause to be aggrieved or affected by it.

It isn't that common for someone to go to the trouble of suing you for making groundless threats. If you don't trouble them again, they may have little to gain by going to the expense of suing you. But it is preferable, if possible, to avoid giving them any basis to do so. There are three ways to avoid making an unjustified or groundless threat.

Write a notification letter

If you are worried about the strength of your case or that you may not be able to afford the costs of suing the infringers, send out a notification letter rather than

---

Case Study Martin

Martin believes that a furniture store in his local town shopping centre is selling a magazine rack that is similar to his own registered design, although it does differ in some respects. He decides to try to frighten off the store from selling any more of the competing products. He sends a demand letter to the furniture store saying they must stop selling the offending item and warning them that if they do not stop, he will sue them for design infringement. He gets no reply from the store. But one week later he receives a letter from the solicitors for the wholesaler who supplied the offending magazine racks.

As a result of Martin's letter, the store has cancelled orders for 20 of the planters. The wholesaler is 'aggrieved' by the threats and is now threatening to sue Martin for making unjustified threats to its customers.

the demand letter (see below). This is a simple letter that merely notifies the recipient that you have a registered trade mark, design or patent and which gives the details of the IP right in question, such as the registered number.

As long as the notification contains nothing else in the way of wording that could be construed as a threat, you can send it without risking a counter-attack for unjustified threats. Just notifying someone that you have a particular right is fine. If they did not know about your IP rights before, it might prompt them to stop. Or the mere fact that they have received the notification may be enough to worry them into desisting for fear of being sued further down the line.

Example of a notification letter

Dear Sirs

UK Patent No. 00999999 – for pushchair hinge mechanism

We have noticed that you are selling folding pushchairs in your shop.

We are the registered proprietor of the above UK patent for a pushchair hinge mechanism under No. 00999999. The details of the patent can be found at http://gb.espacenet.com.

Yours faithfully,

If available, rely on passing off or copyright infringement

You can rely solely on a right that cannot give rise to a claim for unjustified threats. For example, if someone is using a sign similar to your trade marked logo, you could avoid mention of your trade mark and rely on copyright infringement, since threats of copyright infringement proceedings are not actionable as unjustified threats.

Carefully word your demand letter

The third, but often best, option is to word your demand letter so that it falls within the exceptions to the unjustified threats provisions. You may need to consult a lawyer if you are unsure of how to do this, but sometimes the scenario you are faced with will make it fairly easy.

The unjustified threats legislation specifically says that threats made in relation to doing certain things are not actionable. It cannot be an unjustified threat to:

- **Threaten someone in relation to importing goods** under a trade mark or importing goods incorporating a protected design.
- **Warn someone about being sued for providing services** under a particular mark.

So, for example, if the person you are writing to is providing services, as long as you confine your trade mark complaint to a complaint about their use to promote their services, you have nothing to worry about. Alternatively, if someone says on their website that they are importing the offending items, you can just complain in your letter about their importation of the goods.

❝Ensure you word your demand letter so that it falls within the exceptions of the unjustified threats provisions. ❞

SENDING OUT THE DEMAND LETTER

You have gathered your evidence, considered the merits of the case and prepared your demand letter. You are content that the threat you will be making is not unjustified or you have concluded that even if it is, you are prepared to take that risk. Now you must send out the letter.

Before doing so (and especially where you are dealing with a large organisation), it is important to try to identify the correct person or department to who your letter should be sent. You do not want it disappearing within a big company or being misdirected to the wrong person.

These days, a lot of communication is by email and, to a lesser extent, via fax. Wherever possible, it is a good idea to combine posting your demand letter with a communication by one or other of these means. If you fax a letter, you have a confirmation page to prove it was successfully transmitted. If you email it, your 'sent' item will carry a time and date stamp showing when it was sent. If you do not have a 'bounce back', the chances are the email was successfully transmitted. Special delivery post is another option.

WHAT IF YOU HAVE NO REPLY?

If you receive no reply to your letter, there may be any number of reasons why. It doesn't always mean that your letter is being ignored. Before taking the drastic step of launching an infringement claim or incurring the costs of seeing a solicitor, it may be worth sending a chaser, just in case.

As a result of the demand letter, you will either open up a process of negotiation that will resolve the dispute before trial or you will have to issue proceedings in an effort to persuade the infringer to stop (see pages 199–202).

RESOLVING DISPUTES OUT OF COURT

The best result from your demand letter is where the party you have warned agrees to modify their activities to your satisfaction and to confirm that they will

❝ Settling disputes without going to court is bound to be cheaper. ❞

not repeat the offending behaviour. Even better is where you can extract some money from them in return for lifting the threat of legal action. Settling disputes without resort to the court is bound to be cheaper than issuing proceedings.

Resolving disputes before issuing proceedings

If the party makes an offer or responds to an offer you have made, you need to decide whether it goes far enough or whether you need to push for a better offer. If your letter has resulted in them putting on hold the infringing activity, the immediate pressure is off and the parties have more time to reach an agreement.

Disputes vary in terms of the issues; their complexity; the relative strengths of the parties' legal cases and financial resources, and the personalities of the individuals involved. In short, it is not possible to set out a definitive guide to all the tactics and scenarios that you might encounter.

You need to give the other party an incentive to settle. That means that they will be better off taking the deal on offer than dragging the dispute out further or ending up in court. Generally, avoid making demands that are unrealistic and that exceed the best possible outcome you could possibly achieve in court. Ultimately, if the case does go to court, you may need to be seen as having been reasonable or you may be penalised on costs.

Some further general guidance that applies to all situations is set out overleaf.

The without prejudice rule

The without prejudice rule means that parties can make private concessions about their case or the remedies they are prepared to accept at the same time as pursuing the dispute. So if you do not want the court to know about something, it should go in a without prejudice letter. It is important to remember, however, that merely putting 'without prejudice' on a letter does not make it such. The substance of what is in the letter is what counts – not the label applied to it.

It is also possible to use the heading 'without prejudice except as to costs' on a letter. This type of correspondence is used where you want the court to take that correspondence into account when it is awarding costs – but only after it has dealt with liability.

In each case, a without prejudice or a without prejudice except as to costs letter should be a separate one to any open correspondence about the case. It should never be included as part of another letter.

To help you, examples of invalid and valid without prejudice letters are set out below and opposite.

Example of a letter incorrectly headed 'without prejudice'

Without prejudice
Dear Sirs

Infringement of registered design No. 00999999 for magazine rack

We have received your letter threatening to bring proceedings against us for design infringement.

We do not accept any of your allegations and have no intention of agreeing to any of your demands. We have only sold 39 of the products in question and have 60 left in stock. We will be selling those if we can. It is possible that once we have done so we will not order any more but if we want to order more we will consider ourselves free to do so.

Yours faithfully,

Example of a without prejudice letter

Dear Sirs
Without prejudice

Infringement of design No. 99999999 for magazine rack

As you know, you have threatened to issue proceedings against us for registered design infringement because of our sale of magazine racks, which you say infringe your registered design. You have threatened to claim up to £50,000 in damages plus an injunction against us and all your legal costs.

We deny your allegations. However, in order to resolve the dispute before proceedings are started and to minimise the costs on each side, we are prepared to make the following offer of settlement:

1.   after 60 days from the date of this letter ('the end date'), we will stop selling the disputed magazine racks at our stores;

2.   in the meantime, we confirm that we will not dispose of, sell or transfer any of the disputed items to a third party;

3.   within 14 days of the end date we will destroy all the remaining unsold racks in our possession or control;

4.   we will pay you within 14 days of the date of this letter, the sum of £1,500 towards your legal costs but no damages.

The above terms shall be in full and final settlement of our dispute. This offer is open for acceptance until [ ] .

Yours faithfully,

IF YOU RECEIVE A DEMAND LETTER

It is perfectly possible that you or your business will find yourself under attack for allegedly infringing someone else's IP rights.

If you find yourself in this situation, you need to carry out pretty much the same exercise as you would when you are considering bringing a claim against someone else. You should investigate the activity that has led to the complaint, analyse the IP rights being relied upon by the claimant and form an assessment as to where you stand on the merits. You can then decide what your strategy for the dispute will be. Are you happy to stop what you are doing? Is it important that you do not back down? Is there a compromise that you could live with to avoid court action? Or is the claimant's case very weak, in which case you may be able to beat it off?

Having weighed up all these matters, write back to the party making the threats and tailor that response to your strategy. If you wish to put out settlement feelers, you can make use of the without prejudice rule (see pages 196–7 where sample letters are also provided) to make an offer to the claimant, while robustly defending yourself against the claims made in an open letter.

FORMALISING THE SETTLEMENT

If you are able to reach a settlement, it is important that the terms agreed are reflected in an exchange of letters or in a separate written agreement that is clear in scope and effect. The settlement agreement should do the following:

- **Clearly identify the parties covered** by the agreement.
- **Summarise the activity** that has led to the dispute.
- **Set out what each party has agreed to do** and clearly identify any IP right that is the subject of those obligations.
- **If any payments of money are to be made,** stipulate a time period for payment.
- **State that the agreement is in full and final settlement** of the matters in dispute.
- **Be dated and signed by** or on behalf of all the parties.

The settlement agreement is a contract between the parties. If a party breaks the terms of that contract, they can be sued for breach of contract. This may be easier than suing again for infringement of an IP right.

If the other party is represented by solicitors, they will almost certainly be incurring legal costs and may look to you to recover those costs. If you are unsure of your position, seek advice from solicitors. If your position is weak, the sooner you resolve the dispute the better. Otherwise, the eventual costs you may have to pay will simply escalate.

Issuing proceedings

If, despite your demand letter, the infringer will not comply with your demands, you may be left with no option but to issue infringement proceedings. This is a significant step. If you later decide to withdraw your proceedings, you cannot just drop them unless you have agreed with the other party about their costs.

COSTS

Besides weighing up your chances of winning the case, one of the most important factors you will need to consider are the costs of litigation.

IP litigation – especially patent litigation – is not a good place for a do-it-yourself approach. Although there are some straightforward cases, a lot of the time, such cases will involve not only contested issues of fact but also contested issues of law. You will inevitably put yourself at a huge disadvantage if you do not receive proper legal advice and guidance during the process (whether as claimant or defendant). Ultimately, it can end up costing more to try to go it alone than if you had consulted professional advisers in the first place.

Conditional fee agreements (CFAs)

Unlike in the US, it remains illegal in the UK for solicitors to charge for a case on the basis of taking a percentage of any damages awarded in a case (known as working on a 'contingency fee basis').

Case Study Andy

Andy has a trade mark that he believes is being infringed by a large internet service provider. He undertakes research and this strengthens his view that his rights are being violated. He does not take legal advice and issues proceedings. The defendant instructs solicitors to defend the claim, who warn Andy in writing that his case is misconceived and that if he does not withdraw, an application will be made to summarily dispose of the claim.

Andy refuses to back down. The defendant applies for judgment against him and Andy loses. As a result, he is faced with a costs bill of £90,000 plus VAT by the successful defendants.

❝ Many IP cases involve not only contested issues of fact but also those of law. You need to take proper legal advice. ❞

However, solicitors are allowed to work on the basis of a CFA, the so-called 'no win, no fee'. Conditional fees involve the solicitors charging only if they win the case (whether defending or prosecuting it). However, in return for shouldering the risk the solicitors are allowed to charge a significant uplift on their normal fees of up to 100 per cent in the event of a successful outcome. Solicitors will usually only take on a case on this basis if they consider that there are good prospects of success.

When instructing solicitors to advise you about IP infringements, it is worth enquiring about CFAs and whether they will act on that basis. However, you do need to consider the pros and cons carefully (see below).

'After the event' insurance

It is possible to take out 'after the event' insurance to guard against the possibility of having to pay the legal costs of the other party in the event the case is lost. Your solicitor should advise you about this and be able to refer you to possible insurers if you decide to take out such insurance. What usually happens is that your solicitor will brief the insurer about the case and, if

The pros and cons of a CFA	
Pros	**Cons**
• Enables you to avoid having to meet substantial legal costs as your case progresses.	• If you achieve a 'win' in your case, your legal bill will be much higher – possibly double – what it would otherwise have been on a non-CFA basis.
• Limits or avoids altogether your liability to pay your own legal costs should your case be unsuccessful.	
• If combined with 'after the event' insurance cover, you may be able to limit or avoid the risk of having to meet the other party's legal costs should your case fail.	• If your opponent does not have the means to meet your legal costs, you may then have to pick up that large bill yourself.
• The fear of being at risk of paying the uplifted costs of a CFA can sometimes persuade the other party to negotiate a settlement.	• If costs are assessed by the court, the amount you are allowed to claim from the losing party may be significantly less than the amount you owe your lawyers under the CFA.
	• In IP cases, very often the damages are not especially great and so there is a greater danger that you will have to foot the bill for irrecoverable costs yourself.

the insurer is willing to provide cover, no premium will be payable for the insurance unless and until the case is concluded successfully. The idea is that the premium (or a large part of it) is then hopefully recovered from the unsuccessful party.

THE LITIGATION PROCESS

It is beyond the scope of this book to examine the litigation process in any real detail, but in broad terms, the process is as follows:

- **Proceedings are started** by issuing a 'claim form' document at court and paying the relevant court fee (which can be a few hundred pounds to a couple of thousand). The claim form is accompanied by a **particulars of claim** document that sets out a summary of what the claimant's case is and what he or she is seeking.
- **If the defendant wishes to contest the case,** he or she must file an acknowledgment of service within 14 days of service of the proceedings and file a **defence document** within a further 14 days.
- **The parties must then complete allocation questionnaires** and send them to the court.
- **The court sets a timetable** (or there is a **case management hearing**), which stipulates the time periods for each procedural stage through to trial and the scope of evidence that may be used.
- **The parties go through the process of disclosure,** under which all relevant documents for or against the parties have to be mutually disclosed. If the case continues, this is where costs can really start to accelerate rapidly.
- **Written witness statements,** results of surveys or experiments and any expert reports are prepared and exchanged by the parties.
- **The trial then takes place,** after which the judge delivers a judgment.

Jargon buster

Allocation questionnaire Litigation in England and Wales is divided into three 'tracks', depending largely on the size and subject matter of the claim. The allocation questionnaire is a form that the parties are required to send to the court to enable it to allocate the case to the appropriate 'track'

Case management hearing This is the name given to a hearing at which the court and the parties decide various housekeeping-type issues relating to a case and manage its progress

Particulars of claim and defence When a claim is started, the claimant serves a document called a particulars of claim on the defendant, which sets out a summary of the claim. These must be answered within a set time by the defendant who files a defence to the particulars of claim

Summary judgment A process for determining summarily a particular issue in a case or the whole case so that it doesn't have to go through the whole litigation process to trial. Summary judgment (and 'striking out', which is very similar) are only suitable where the issues are clear cut and can be demonstrated by written evidence, rather than cross examination of witnesses such as at trial

The process from start to finish may take as much as a year or even longer to complete, depending on the complexity of the case. There may also be contested hearings along the way at which the court has to make interim rulings. However, in some cases, where the claim or defence stands no real prospect of success, it is possible to shorten the process by applying for a **summary judgment**. If successful, this will bring the proceedings to an end and so cut out all the remaining stages of the process after the filing of the defence.

APPEALS

It is also possible for cases to be appealed if the parties do not like the result. However, because much IP law in the UK is now created in Europe, very often if there is a point of law under appeal, it has to be determined by the European Court of Justice. This may cause the matter to drag on for years before being resolved.

ENFORCEMENT

Just because a judgment is obtained, it may not be the end of the matter. If, for example, a party is ordered to pay money to the claimant in the judgment, but fails to pay, the onus is on the claimant to bring enforcement proceedings to recover the money. Similarly, if someone breaches the terms of an injunction, you cannot call the police to help you. You have to bring legal proceedings for contempt of court against the defaulter.

> **The process can take longer than a year from start to finish, but it is possible to shorten proceedings in some cases by applying for a summary judgment.**

Glossary

Account of profits: A remedy in IP infringement proceedings whereby the infringing party is required to pay over to the successful claimant the profits it has earned from infringing the IP rights in question.

Allocation questionnaire: Litigation in England and Wales is divided into three 'tracks', depending largely on the size and subject matter of the claim. The allocation questionnaire is a form that the parties are required to send to the court to enable it to allocate the case to the appropriate track.

Artistic work: A category of copyright work including such things as photographs, graphic works and sculptures.

Assignment: A transfer of title or ownership in property (including intellectual property) from one party to another party.

Business angel: An individual who invests (either on their own or in combination with others) in new or developing businesses and who may provide assistance above and beyond their financial contribution.

Business Link: A service to help businesses, which is funded by the Government through the Department for Business, Enterprise and Regulatory Reform.

CE marking: A quality mark borne by certain categories of products to evidence their compliance with the requirements of various EU Directives for types of goods.

Civil infringement action: Legal action for infringement of IP rights can be brought by the rights holder against the wrongdoer in the civil courts. The kinds of remedies available in such an action would be an injunction, damages or an account of profits.

Civil Procedure Rules (CPR): The procedural rules that govern all aspects of litigation in the courts of England and Wales.

Claimant: The party making a claim in legal proceedings (formerly known as the 'plaintiff').

Community design: A right that offers legal protection to designs throughout the EU provided they meet certain qualifying criteria. Registered and unregistered Community designs offer different levels of protection.

Community trade mark: A right that offers legal protection to trade marks throughout the EU provided they meet certain qualifying criteria and are registered with OHIM.

Company secretary: An officer of a company who is responsible for maintaining statutory books and records.

203

Competition law: Laws that operate in the UK and EU to combat unfair and anti-competitive practices and agreements.

Conditional fee agreement (CFA): A retainer with a lawyer, which allows the lawyer to charge an uplift on his or her normal fees in the event of a successful outcome to a case.

Copyright: A species of IP right that protects certain types of creative works from being copied or dealt with without the permission of the copyright owner.

Copyright Designs & Patents Act 1988: The main legislation governing copyright law in the UK and the law of UK unregistered designs.

Corporation Tax: The tax paid by companies on company profits.

Cost pricing: Setting the price of goods or services by reference to the cost of providing them rather than the value they are perceived to have by potential customers.

Counterclaim: In some cases, a defendant to a set of legal proceedings may have a claim of its own to make against the claimant, in which case it may file that claim as a counterclaim in the same proceedings.

Damages: A sum of money the court awards to the successful claimant to compensate him or her for losses caused by infringements of his or her rights by the defendant.

Defendant: The party who is the subject of a claim in legal proceedings.

Demand letter: A piece of correspondence sent by a potential claimant to a potential defendant to warn them of a legal dispute and which threatens legal action if the dispute is not resolved (often referred to as a 'letter before action').

Design document: A document embodying the design, such as a picture of how a film prop should look or a design drawing showing the appearance and dimensions of a design for a car.

Design right: The term used to describe unregistered designs protected by UK or EU legislation.

Direct marketing: The practice of sending unsolicited mail ('junk mail'), emails or making unsolicited calls to potential customers.

Directors: Officers of a company – usually employees – who have special status. They not only exercise certain powers conferred on them by the company's constitution to run the affairs of the company, but they have duties and responsibilities imposed on them by company law. All companies have to have at least one director.

Distributor: An entity that is appointed by a brand owner to service a territory and which buys goods from the brand owner and then sells or promotes and distributes them in its appointed territory.

Dividends: Payments made by a company to its shareholders. Usually they are linked to a company's profits. The more profit a company makes, the higher the dividend payments it makes.

Domain name: The internet address that forms part of a website address or URL. Domain names are formed of a name and an extension, such as .com, .co.uk and .biz.

Equity finance: Money raised by issuing shares in a business.

EU Directive: A Directive is a piece of legislation made at EU level that obliges all EU Member States to introduce their own domestic legislation so as to implement the provisions of the Directive.

EU Regulation: A Regulation is a piece of legislation made at EU level that has direct legal effect in all EU Member States.

European Economic Area (EEA): The area that is made up of all the EU countries plus Iceland, Liechtenstein and Norway.

European Patent Convention (EPC): The EPC was created in 1973 (and revised in 2007). It established a system of European patents whereby through a single filing, applicants can apply for a European patent that has effect under the national laws of any European states stipulated in the application. As at December 2008 there are 34 countries covered by the EPC.

European Patent Office (EPO): Administers the filing and registration of European patents.

European Union (EU): The union of countries (currently 27) who are signatories of the Treaty of Rome and who have agreed to participate in and be governed under the jurisdiction of EU institutions.

Exclusive distributor/licence: A contract under which the distributor/licensee is given the exclusive rights to something (such as copyright) in a territory to the exclusion of everyone else – including the rights holder who grants the licence appoints the distributor.

Franchise: A format for running a business under which a business (the 'franchisor') appoints other businesses or individuals as 'franchisees' to operate independent businesses adopting the franchisor's trading style and operational procedures in return for a fee.

'Get up': A legal phrase that describes how a product looks in its packaging. For example, the 'get up' of a can of coke is the colouring and design of the can, the 'get up' of a Jif lemon is the yellow lemon-shaped container that the Jif lemon juice comes in.

Gross sales: The total of the value of sales achieved before deduction of any costs or expenses.

Informed user: A fictional person through whose eyes the court judges whether a design has individual character. The informed user is not an expert in the relevant field, but nor is he or she an ordinary consumer. Rather, the informed user is a person in between those extremes who is familiar with designs in the sector concerned.

Infringement: Breach of rights under the applicable IP legislation.

Injunction: An order of the court requiring the party concerned to either do or refrain from doing a particular act. Breach of an injunction is a serious matter and is a contempt of court punishable by imprisonment, a fine or both.

Intellectual property (IP): The legally enforceable rights that can exist in relation to various creative and otherwise intangible things, such as copyright, designs, trade marks, patents, designs and business goodwill.

Intellectual Property Office (IPO): Formerly the UK Intellectual Property Office (UKIPO) and before that the Patent Office, this is the UK's agency for administering the system of registered trade marks, UK registered designs and patents.

Invalidity proceedings: Proceedings in which a party disputes the entitlement of another party to own a registered IP right, such as a trade mark, patent or design, on the grounds that the right is defective and should not have been registered.

Invention promoter: An organisation that helps inventors to evaluate whether their inventions are likely to be commercially viable and, if so, to introduce them to businesses that might be interested in exploiting the invention.

Licence: A permission given (often in writing) by a rights owner to someone else ('the licensee') to exercise rights that would otherwise be the exclusive preserve of the rights owner.

Limited company: A corporate entity registered at Companies House that has its own legal personality but which, if it becomes insolvent, does not automatically expose its members or officers to any further liability.

Limited liability: In the context of a limited company, this means that if a company becomes insolvent, its liability to any creditors is limited to the value of its issued share capital.

Manufacturing Advisory Service (MAS): A government-supported body operated under the auspices of BERR.

Net sales: The value of gross sales less costs and expenses (this is usually defined in the licence agreement).

No win, no fee: If you lose the case, you do not have to pay your lawyer's legal bill (although you might still be liable to pay part of the winner's legal costs unless you had insured against them). In a no win, no fee case, if you win your case, your lawyer will normally charge significantly more than if you had been on an ordinary retainer (see also conditional fee agreement).

Non-exclusive distributor/licence: Where the rights holder reserves the right to appoint more than one distributor/licensee in a territory, including selling there itself.

Office for Harmonisation of the Internal Market (OHIM): An EU body based in Alicante, Spain, which administers the operation of the design registration system for Community trade marks and Community designs.

Opposition proceedings: Where a party files for registration of a patent, design or trade mark it is possible for an interested party to oppose the grant of a registered right by filing opposition proceedings with the appropriate administrative office. If the proceedings are successful, it blocks the registration of the disputed right. If the opposition fails, the application will proceed.

Particulars of claim: One of the key documents, along with a claim form, that a claimant needs to file at court and serve on the defendant when starting civil proceedings.

Partnership: A business entity with unlimited liability whereby two or more persons carry on business together with a view to profit.

Passing off: Where a business has acquired a goodwill and reputation in the UK by reference to an identifying name, logo or get up ('identifier'), it can sue other traders for passing off if they damage or threaten to damage that goodwill by trading using a confusingly similar identifier.

Patent: A legal right that protects new inventions, provided they meet certain qualifying criteria.

Patent Co-operation Treaty (PCT): The PCT is an international patent treaty that facilitates the filing of patents by applicants in different countries, via a single application to an administrative body. The priority date of a patent filed under the PCT is recognised by countries who are PCT signatories and the filings proceed as national patents in the countries chosen by the applicant.

Patents Act 1977: The main piece of legislation that governs the workings of patent law in the UK.

Prior Art (designs): The pre-existing designs (which could reasonably have been known about in the European Economic Area by relevant design circles) against which the validity of a protected design is assessed to see if it really is 'new' or has 'individual character'.

Prior Art (patents): The pre-existing state of knowledge, published worldwide (including patents, research data, articles and books) against which an invention is assessed for its novelty and inventiveness. The prior art is relevant to the question of whether or not a patent application should be granted and/or declared invalid.

Priority date: This is generally the date on which the formal application for a patent, registered trade mark or design is first filed with the relevant receiving office – it is the earliest date from which protection starts. The priority date is important because not only does it become the date from which protection starts, but it is also the date at which the validity of a patent, trade mark or design is assessed. This becomes important if it is challenged.

Registered design: A design that enjoys enhanced protection through having been registered with the appropriate administrative agency, such as the IPO or OHIM.

Registered Designs Act 1949: The legislation that governs UK registered design law.

Registered trade mark: A trade mark that has been protected by being registered with the appropriate administrative agency, such as the IPO or OHIM.

Revocation: A registered IP right may in some circumstances cease to be registerable, such as if a registered trade mark is not put to genuine use for a continuous period of five years or more, in which case it may be revoked upon an application to the court.

Royalties: Payments made by someone who has taken a licence from the IP rights owner. Such payments are usually based on a royalty rate, which is often expressed as a percentage of the value of sales.

Royalty-free licence: A licence where no royalties are payable by the licensee.

Sales promotion: A means of promoting goods via some special marketing event, such as a tasting stand in a retail store or a special introductory offer on the product.

Shareholders: Companies are owned by shareholders. They take shares in a company, which rise or fall in value depending on the value of the company. Shareholders ultimately control the company and may receive dividend payments.

Shareholders' agreement: A contract entered into between shareholders in a company, which regulates their business relationship and which may modify the effect, as between them, of what would otherwise be their obligations under company law.

Sole distributor/licence: Where the rights holder agrees to appoint only one distributor/licence in a territory, but reserves its own right to sell goods in that territory too.

Sole trader: Someone who carries on a business unincorporated and who is not in partnership.

State of the art: For the purposes of patent law, this comprises all matter (whether a product, process, information about either, or anything else), which has, at any time before the priority date, been made available to the public (whether in the UK or elsewhere) by written or oral description, by use or in any other way. In other words, 'the state of the art' covers the whole world. If something is already out there in, say, Chile, it can invalidate an application for a patent in the UK.

Sub-licensing of rights: Where a licensee is appointed, that licensee may itself grant a sub-licence to another party to do certain things with the IP rights in order for the licensee to fulfil its obligations under its licence. To ensure the licensee does not breach its agreement with the licensor, the obligations imposed on the sub-licensee should normally mirror the obligations in the main licence.

Summary judgment: A process for determining summarily a particular issue in a case or the whole case so that it doesn't have to go through the whole litigation process to trial. Summary judgment (and 'striking out', which is very similar) is only suitable where the issues are clear cut and can be demonstrated by written evidence, rather than cross examination of witnesses, such as at trial.

Trade Marks Act 1994: The legislation that governs the law of UK registered trade marks.

Trading law: Rules and regulations that apply to the sale of goods or provision of services, including health and safety, labelling and other statutory requirements.

Trading standards: Departments set up by each local authority that are responsible for enforcing trading laws and certain IP laws (such as the criminal infringement provisions of the Trade Marks Act 1994).

Venture capital: Some organisations or wealthy individuals make money available to invest in businesses and business ventures in the hope of making a financial return on their investment.

WHOIS: A term to describe the search facility available at internet registrars that permits members of the public to search for the name and address of the proprietor of domain names.

Without prejudice: Denotes that the contents of a particular communication are aimed at exploring or negotiating a settlement of a dispute and consequently that such communications should not be disclosable in legal proceedings.

Working capital: Finance that is used to fund the running of a business aside from revenues received from its trading activities.

World Intellectual Property Organisation (WIPO): This body, based in Switzerland is responsible for administering certain international systems of IP protection, including international patents, trade marks and designs.

Useful addresses

Advertising Standards Authority
(ASA)
Mid City Place
71 High Holborn
London WC1V 6QT
Tel: 020 7492 2222
www.asa.org.uk

Advisory, Conciliation and Arbitration
Service (ACAS)
Brandon House
180 Borough High Street
London SE1 1LW
Helpline: 08457 47 47 47
www.acas.org.uk

British Business Angels Association
(BBAA)
New City Court
20 St Thomas Street
London SE1 9RS
Tel: 0207 089 2305
www.bbaa.org.uk

British Franchising Association (BFA)
A2 Danebrook Court
Oxford Office Village
Langford Lane
Oxford OX5 1LQ
Tel: 01865 379892
www.thebfa.org

British Standards Institution (BSI)
389 Chiswick High Road
London W4 4AL
Tel: 020 8996 9001
www.bsi-global.com

British Venture Capital Association
(BVCA)
3 Clements Inn
London WC2A 2AZ
Tel: 020 7025 2950
www.bvca.co.uk

Business Link
To find your nearest operator, tel: 0845
600 9 006, www.businesslink.gov.uk
Business Eye (Wales):
Tel: 03000 6 03000,
www.business-support-wales.gov.uk
Business Gateway (Scotland):
Tel: 0845 609 6611, www.bgateway.com
Invest Northern Ireland: www.investni.com

Chartered Institute of Patent
Attorneys (CIPA)
95 Chancery Lane
London WC2A 1DT
Tel: 020 7405 9450
www.cipa.org.uk

Chartered Institute of Public Relations
(CIPR)
32 St James's Square
London SW1Y 4JR
Tel: 020 7766 3333
www.cipr.co.uk

Companies House
Companies House Executive Agency
21 Bloomsbury Street
London WC1B 3XD
Tel: 0303 1234 500
www.companieshouse.gov.uk

Department of Business Enterprise
and Regulatory Reform
Ministerial Correspondence Unit
1 Victoria Street
London SW1H OET
Tel: 020 7215 5000
www.berr.gov.uk

Dun & Bradstreet
35 Wilson Street
London EC2A IPX
Tel: 01628 492000
www.dnb.co.uk
(providers of company information and
credit ratings)

Espacenet
http://gb.espacenet.com

European Patent Office
Austria
Postfach 90
1031 Vienna
Austria
Tel: +43 152126 0
www.epo.org

Belgium
Av. de Cortenbergh, 60
1000 Brussels
Belgium
Tel: +32 2 274 15 90
www.epo.org

Germany
80298 Munich
Germany
Tel: +49 89 2399 0
www.epo.org

10958 Berlin
Germany
Tel: +49 30 25901 0
www.epo.org

Holland
Postbus 5818
2280 HV Rijswijk
The Netherlands
Tel: +31 70340 2040
www.epo.org

Equifax
www.equifax.co.uk
(providers of company information and
credit ratings)

Experion
www.experion.co.uk
(providers of company information and
credit ratings)

Global TGI
Tel: 020 8433 4090
www.tgisurveys.com

Information Commissioner's Office (ICO)
Wycliffe House
Water Lane
Wilmslow
Cheshire SK9 5AF
Tel: 08456 30 60 60
www.ico.gov.uk

Institute of Practitioners in Advertising
(IPA)
44 Belgrave Square
London SW1X 8QS
Tel: 020 7235 7020
www.ipa.co.uk

Institute of Trade Mark Attorneys (ITMA)
ITMA Office
Canterbury House
2–6 Sydenham Rd
Croydon
Surrey CRO 9XE
Tel: 020 8686 2052
www.itma.org.uk

Intellectual Property Office (IPO)
Concept House
Cardiff Road
Newport NP10 8QQ
Tel: 01633 814000
www.ipo.gov.uk

Internet Advertising Bureau (IAB)
14 Macklin Street
London WC2B 5NF
Tel: 020 7050 6969
www.iabuk.net

Knowledge Transfer Partnerships (KTPs)
KTP Programme Office
AEA
Didcot
Oxfordshire OX11 0QJ
Tel: 0870 190 2829
www.ktponline.org.uk

The Law Society
England and Wales
113 Chancery Lane
London WC2A 1PL
Tel: 0870 606 6575
www.lawsociety.co.uk

The Law Society of Scotland
26 Drumsheugh Gardens
Edinburgh EH3 7YR
Tel: 0131 226 7411
www.lawscot.org.uk

The Law Society of Northern Ireland
Law Society House
98 Victoria Street
Belfast BT1 3JZ
Tel: 028 90 2316 14
www.lawsoc-ni.org

Manufacturing Advice Service (MAS)
Tel: 0845 658 9600
www.mas.dti.gov.uk

Market Research Society (MRS)
15 Northburgh Street
London EC1V 0JR
Tel: 020 7490 4911
www.mrs.org.uk

National Federation of Enterprise
Agencies (NFEA)
12 Stephenson Court
Fraser Road
Priory Business Park
Bedford MK44 3WJ
Tel: 01234 831623
www.nfea.com

National Federation of Small Businesses
(NFSB)
Sir Frank Whittle Way
Blackpool Business Park
Blackpool FY4 2FE
Tel: 01253 336000
www.fsb.org.uk

Nominet UK
www.nominet.org.uk
(administers internet domain names for
the UK)

Office for Harmonisation in the Internal
Market (Trade Marks and Designs)
Avenida de Europa, 4
E-03008 Alicante
Spain
Tel: + 34 96 513 9100
www.oami.europa.eu

Office for National Statistics (ONS)
Cardiff Road
Newport NP10 8XG
Tel: 0845 601 3034
www.statistics.gov.uk

Office of Fair Trading (OFT)
Enquiries Unit
Office of Fair Trading
Fleetbank House
2–6 Salisbury Square
London EC4Y 8JX
Tel: 020 7211 8000
www.oft.gov.uk

Office of Public Sector Information (OPSI)
(formerly Her Majesty's Stationery Office)
102 Petty France
London SW1H 9AJ
Tel 020 8876 3444
www.opsi.gov.uk

World Intellectual Property Organisation (WIPO)
34 Chemin des Colombettes
Geneva
Switzerland
Tel: +41 22 338 9111
www.wipo.int

Useful addresses

Index

Index

Which? is the leading independent consumer champion in the UK.
A not-for-profit organisation, we exist to make individuals as powerful as the
organisations they deal with in everyday life. The next few pages give you a
taster of our many products and services. For more information, log onto
www.which.co.uk or call 0800 252 100.

Which? Online

www.which.co.uk gives you access to all Which? content online and much, much more.
It's updated regularly, so you can read hundreds of product reports and Best Buy
recommendations, keep up to date with Which? campaigns, compare products, use our
financial planning tools and search for the best cars on the market. You can also access
reviews from *The Good Food Guide*, register for email updates and browse our online
shop – so what are you waiting for? To subscribe, go to www.which.co.uk.

Which? Money

Whether you want to boost your pension, make your savings work harder or simply need
to find the best credit card, *Which? Money* has the information you need. *Which? Money*
offers you honest, unbiased reviews of the best (and worst) new personal finance deals,
from bank accounts to loans, credit cards to savings accounts. Throughout the magazine
you will find tips and ideas to make your budget go further plus dozens of Best Buys. To
subscribe, go to www.which.co.uk.

Which? Computing

If you own a computer, are thinking of buying one or just want to keep abreast of the
latest technology and keep up with your kids, there's one invaluable source of information
you can turn to – *Which? Computing* magazine. *Which? Computing* offers you honest
unbiased reviews of new technology, problem-solving tips from the experts and
step-by-step guides to help you make the most of your computer. To subscribe, go
to www.which.co.uk.

Which? Books

Other books in this series

Save and Invest

Jonquil Lowe
ISBN: 978 1 84490 044 2
Price £10.99

Save and Invest is a detailed guide to all saving and investment avenues suitable for those approaching the markets for the first time and those seeking to improve their portfolio. Jonquil Lowe, an experienced investment analyst, introduces the basics of understanding risk and suggests popular starter investments. Many types of savings accounts are closely analysed, along with more complex investment options, such as venture capital trusts, high-income bonds, hedge funds and spread betting.

Wills and Probate

Paul Elmhirst
ISBN: 978 1 84490 033 6
Price £10.99

Wills and Probate provides clear and easy-to-follow guidance on the main provisions to make in a will and the factors you should consider when drafting these. The second part of the book provides step-by-step guidance on probate, making the process as straightforward and trouble-free as possible. By being aware of key changes and revisions and avoiding the problems and pitfalls, you can limit delays, avoid disputes and save tax.

Working for Yourself

Mike Pywell and Bill Hilton
ISBN: 978 1 84490 040 4
Price £10.99

Most of us want the freedom offered by self-employment. *Working for Yourself* will help you make that jump out of the rat race. Covering tips on freelancing, consultancy and contract work, this book provides all the financial and legal information to get you off to the best start possible.

Which? Books

Other books in this series

Finance Your Retirement
Jonquil Lowe
ISBN: 978 1 84490 057 2
Price £10.99

Finance Your Retirement is the essential step-by-step guide to a secure retirement, providing advice on saving for your pension, whether to opt for an annuity, how to access your money if you retire abroad and the basics of Inheritance Tax. There are helpful tips for maximising your budget using state benefits and investments, such as unit trusts and OEICs, plus guidance on how to make your property work for you.

Managing Your Debt
Phillip Inman
ISBN: 978 1 84490 041 1
Price £10.99

Managing Your Debt is a practical and straightforward guide to managing your finances and getting your money, and your life, back on track. Phillip Inman, the *Guardian*'s business correspondent covers a wide range of topics including how to identify and deal with priority debts, the best way to make a debt-management plan, who to contact and what to expect should you ever face bankruptcy or an individual voluntary agreement.

Money Saving Handbook
Tony Levene
ISBN: 978 1 84490 048 0
Price £10.99

From low-cost air travel and zero per cent finance to cheap mobile phone tariffs, the list of financial products is endless and the good deals are harder to find. The *Guardian*'s personal finance expert, Tony Levene, separates the cons from the bargains and explains how to avoid hidden charges and penalty fees. *Money Saving Handbook* is the key to becoming smarter with your money.

Which? Books

Which? Books provide impartial, expert advice on everyday matters from finance to law, property to major life events. We also publish the country's most trusted restaurant guide, *The Good Food Guide*. To find out more about Which? Books, log on to www.which.co.uk or call 01903 828557.

" Which? tackles the issues that really matter to consumers and gives you the advice and active support you need to buy the right products. **"**